SEGRETO ITALIANO

SEGRETO ITALIANO

SECRET RECIPES & FAVORITE ITALIAN DISHES

by
Daniel Bellino-Zwicke

Segreto Italiano
- Secret Recipes & Favorite Italian Dishes

Copyright Daniel Bellino-Zwicke 2014
All rights reserved.
First Edition
Broadway Fifth Press, New York, NY 2014

First Edition Broadway Fifth Press 2014
New York, New York
Cover Design Daniel Bellino Zwicke
Cover photo property of Daniel Bellino Zwicke
First Published by Broadway Fifth Press 2014
Library of Congress Cataloging-in-Publication
Data, Zwicke Bellino, Daniel
Segreto Italiano
ISBN- 10: 1500727237
ISBN- 13: 978-1500727239
1. Zwicke Bellino, Daniel, Cooks – New
York(State)—New York—Nonfiction, I Title

Dedicated to Lucia Bellino
Josephina Bellino
Fran Bellino
Helen Cavallo

All My Fellow Italian-Americans
Who Love This Food
These Dishes
and
These Recipe
And The Spirit
of The
Italian-American Table

Mangia Bene!!!

CONTENTS

CONTENTS

CONTENTS

The Recipes & This Book

Yes, the recipes and this book. The name should tell you something, Segreto Italiano (Italian Secrets), Secret Recipes and Favorite Italian Dishes. And it's just that. Some of the dishes are secret or rare, the rest Italian favorites, as well as favorites of any and all people who love Italian, and Italian-American food. And isn't that *everyone?*

Some recipes are secret like Danny's Bolognese and Pasta Segrete. Many are world famous, like Clemenza's Mob War Sunday Sauce, while others are famous within smaller circles, yet famous and equally tasty never-the-less.

Why do you say Italian and Italian-American you might ask? Aren't they the same? Well, Yes and No. Italian-American is mostly Italian Food. About 90% ... But there are some differences, most of them slight, some not. They're been a great debate, mostly by people who don't know as much about food as their bloated heads think they do. Is Italian-American really a cuisine, and some of them may so no. But yes it is. All cuisines grow and change over times, and new one develop. Italian-American is a cuisine, and a legitimate one at that. What it is, a cuisine based on the cuisine and foods of Italy. It stems from Italy, Italian immigrants to the U.S.A. and the way these immigrants made their regional Italian dishes hear in America, and created a few new one out of necessity and circumstances. They mostly cooked the dishes of their hometowns and regions. They'd make them the same ways. Some they might change a bit, and some we be created new, by immigrants in their homes or in restaurants. Dishes like Veal Parmigiano (Veal Parmesan) and Chicken Parmigiano were created here. So were Spaghetti & Meatballs as they say, as well as "Gravy," a.k.a. Sunday Sauce which was adapted and embellished from the famous Neapolitan dish of Ragu Napoletano. Ragu Napoletano is made by braised one large piece of beef in a tomato sauce for a long time. This piece of beef imparts beef flavor into the tomato sauce. When finished, the piece of meat is removed from the sauce. You cook some pasta and serve it as a first course napped in the tomato sauce, minus the meat. The beef is sliced and serve with potatoes or polenta as the main course, and napped with just a little of the sauce. Italian-Americans who came to America back at the turn of the 1900 were quite poor, and many might have only had meat a few times a year.

When they came to America and worked as laborers, they were not rich, but America, a land of plenty, even with their small salaries, these immigrants could afford meat a couple times a week instead of just a few times a year. These immigrants in New York, Boston, Baltimore, New Orleans, wherever started creating some hybrid Italian dishes that stemmed from their roots (Italian) and their food. The greatest hybrid Italian-American dish is none other than Sunday Sauce, or as some call it, simply Gravy. These early Italian immigrants and 1st Generation Italian-Americans created one of the culinary worlds greatest dishes ever; Gravy, Sundays Sauce, some just call it "Sauce." The Gravy is made with a tomato sauce that has two or more meat products braised in it. Usually it simmers for hours on the back of the stove. The meats used and the most popular kind of Sunday Sauce (Gravy) is made with; Sausage, Meatballs, and Braciole. As you will see later, Pete Clemenza's famous *sauce* from Francis Ford Coppola's Italian-American Classic film "The Godfather" is made with just Meatballs and Sausages. Some make it with Pork Neck, Sausage, and Meatballs. Some throw in some chicken, and some, as me for one like to make or Sunday Sauce Gravy with Pork Spare Ribs thrown in the mix. Dam that's tasty.

So you have Secret Sauce and other *Secret Recipes*, some rare ones like; Goulash Triestino, and family recipes like; Uncle Pete's Baked Rabbit or Uncle Vinny's Sausage & Beans. You have your favorites, like; Spaghetti & Meatballs, Lasagna, Pasta Fagoli (Pasta Fazool), Clams Casino, Shrimp Scampi and more. The Secret ones, like; Salsa Segrete all Gino's and Danny's Bolognese. You should pay $100 just for this last one alone, which I kept Secret for many years, but now, in kindness and good will to my fellow man, I'm giving it to you. And it's "Practically Free." How's that for a deal? And what about Gino's Salsa Segrete? Free too. Hey, "I'm getting Robbed here!"

Well, That's Italian! Italian-American, and it's all so tasty and spirit lifting. Make these recipes, perfect them, they're a treasure trove of Italian Favorites and Secret ones too. "Mangia Bene e Sempre Avere Buono Tempi," (Eat Well & Always Have Good Times).

SEGRETI
"Secrets"

Segreto? It's *secret* in Italian. I got the idea for the book one day, well not the idea, but inspiration I'd say. I was thinking about one of our all time favorites restaurant, the food, the ambiance and all the fun we'd had there over the years. Many wonderful meals with family and friend, no foes. Dinners with Cousin Joe, Sister Barbara, Brother Michael, and Jimmy. Oh, the food was wonderful, all the great Italian Classics of good old Italian-American Red Sauce Joints of which this one, was one of the best. The classics, like: Baked Clams, Stuffed Artichokes, Spaghetti & Meatballs, Linguine with Clam Sauce, Chicken Parmigiano, Veal Marsala & Milanese, Chicken Cacctiatore, Ossobuco, Cannolis, Spumoni, and-on-and-on. I think you get the picture. Lots of good, affordable Italian Wine, the affable waiter, the phone booth, and the Zebra Wall Paper. If you were a regular their, from the last sentence, you the place I'm talking about. Yes Gino's! Our beloved Gino's of Lexington Avenue. Sadly they closed a few years ago. But we still have the memories of so many festive meals. Happy times, good eats.

I discovered the wonders of Gino's and first brought my cousin Joe there in 1999. The place was thrilling in that, when you walked in, you felt you were in the perfect place. Gino's is charged with energy by its wonderful clientele, well-healed regulars who have been going there for years, they know the Maitre'd, the waiters and other customers, and likewise the waiters, bartender, and maitre'd know them. The first time you walk in, you feel that, and want to be a part of it. We did. Back then, Joe and I used to go out to eat together all the time, at least once a week. Joe knew about food, but not to the extent that I did. Joe would come in every week or so, and his driver would drive us around town. He'd pick me up early evening for a night of feasting and good times. We'd often eat at a couple different place. We'd have our main dinner and maybe a little bite to eat when we first went for cocktails to start the night off. As I said, Joe loved eating, and knew quite a bit, but as much as he knew, it wasn't a third of what I knew about food, wine, and restaurants, and especially the restaurant, bar, and night club scene in New York. I was teaching Joe the ropes, so-to-speak, and Joe was an eager student. We had quite a lot of fun those few years, with dinners at Gino's, Elio's (Mondays for Lasagna), Da Silvanos's,

Bar Pitti, The Waverly Inn, Minetta Tavern, cocktails at Pegu and Temple Bar, and way too many other places to name right here. We did New York, we did it all!

Back to Gino's. So I had passed by Gino's any number of times, but never went in to check it out. I was a downtowner, and that's where we did most of our eating, with an occasional trip midtown or other local if a place peaked our interest. So I did finally walk into Gino's one day. I had to check it out. When I did, as I've already said, I walked in the door and immediately felt the energy of the place. Gino's was packed, full of life and vibrant, and I knew I wanted to be there. I didn't eat there right then and there, I was scouting the place out, but I knew I would be back. So I called Joe up and told him all about the place. It sounded great to Joe, this type of place was right up his alley, as it was mine. So Joe said yes, let's check it out on our next night out.

Our first ever trip to Gino's was a few nights later. Joe packed me up at my place in Greenwich Village. I got in the car, as usual, we had a little discussion on what we'd be doing.

We mapped out the night of eating and drinking, good times. We talked and decided to head over to Otto Enoteca for a bottle of wine and some Salumi before heading up town to Gino's and our main dinner of the night. Joe loved Otto, and I was a fan too, so we headed to Otto.

Well, we went to Otto, drank a little wine, had some Testa, Mortadella, and Prosciutto, and it was on to Gino's. Back in the car, and Ziggy (our driver) drove us up to Lexington Avenue, across the street from Bloomingdale's to Gino's. We were excited as we walked up to the restaurant and through the door. The place was packed and super-charged. We loved it. The Maitre'd greeted us with the first of many warm welcomes. We were in like Flynn. We sat down at a nice table in the middle of the restaurant. We were happy campers. As happy as can be, for we sensed a wonderful meal ahead. Our hunch would turn out to be just right. A waiter came to our table, greeted us a warm welcome, gave us a wine list and menus, and asked what type of water we wanted. As always, we got a bottle of flat water. Joe gave me the wine list as he usually does and told me to pick something out. I looked over the reasonably priced list and picked out a tried and true wine from my good friend Luigi Cappellini in Greve. The wine, a bottle of Verrazzano Chianti Classico. The waiter went to get the wine, and Joe and I looked over the menu. We were happy to see a great old school Italian menu. The Red Sauce kind of a good old classic Italian-American joint, of which there used to be many, but at this point of time, far fewer. They had; Shrimp Cocktail, Baked Clams, Hot Antipasto, Clams Posillipo, Spaghetti Vongole, Lasagna, Canneloni, Veal Parm, Veal Milanese, Eggplant Parmigiano, Shrimp Fra Diavolo, Veal Marsala, Scampi, and all the usual suspects. We were in heaven, and it was heard narrowing down what to eat.

One dish really caught our attention, and especially Joe, who although I love my pasta, Joe had has me beat, he's the pasta freak. Freak in a good way that is. The dish was Pasta Segrete (Pasta w/Secret Sauce), and us intrigued.

The waiter brought the bottle of Chianti, opened it, and we were on our way. I ripped off a piece of bread and ate it. So, we decided on the menu. We order a Shrimp Cocktail and Baked Clams Oreganata to start. We would share these two antipasto items, then move on to the Primi, the pasta course. We decided on, and just had to have the Pasta Segrete, a half order each. We both love Veal Milanese (Frank Sinatra's favorite), and as we were having antipasto, and pasta, as well as a couple desserts, we decided on one Veal Milanese to split for the main course, thus leaving room for some tasty desserts we knew Gino's would have. We talked with the our waiter about the menu, and he agreed that we had chosen wisely, and that one Milanese would be fine, so we could eat dessert and he'd help us pick the two best later.

So we drank wine, and nibble on the bread, chatted and waited in anticipation for the antipasto to arrive. I love Shrimp Cocktail since childhood and don't always eat it all that much these days, so it's always a special treat. The Baked Clams and the Shrimp Cocktail came and were a great way to start the meal. The wine was great. Hey it's Castello Verrazzano!

So now, we were really excited. This mysterious *Pasta Segrete* was about to come out. You can get the Secret Sauce with whatever Pasta you like, Spaghetti, Raviolis, Tagiolini, Penne, Gnocchi, or Rigatoni. Joe and I both love Rigatoni, so that's what we went for, two half portions of Rigatoni Segrete. Well, the waiter brought us our Pasta with Secret Sauce. Guess what! It was outrageous, and we just loved it. Joe went crazy, and could stop talking about it, and it was just a couple weeks before he'd have to go back and get another *"Fix."* Yes the Pasta with the Secret Sauce did not disappoint. We loved it, and would be back for many more bowls.

We finished the Pasta, grudgingly so, as we didn't want the experience to end, "It was that good!" We waited a few minutes for the Veal Milanese. It came out, and we could tell just by looking at it, that it would be great. For those of you who might not know, Veal Milanese is one of Italy's most famous a classic of all dishes. It's a Veal Chop that's pounded thin, breaded with breadcrumbs and fried and tipped with a Salad of Arugala and Tomato. The dish is simple, simply delicious when done right. Veal Milanese was one of Frank Sinatra's all-time favorite dish, along with Spaghetti Meatballs, and Clams Posillipo. Frank used to get it often at his favorite of all restaurants, Patsy's of West 56th Street, just 10 blocks from Gino's. Both old-school Italian Joints were amongst Frank's favorites. Patsy's was Frank's # 1 favorite, but Gino's wasn't far behind, and Ol' Bue Eyes ate there many times over the years. Anyway, the Veal Milanese was just perfect and we thoroughly enjoyed it. Yes, life is good at times like these.

We finished our Veal Milanese, and it was now time to think about desserts. I love sweets and so does Joe, so he said we gotta get two. The waiter told us the Tiramisu was "The Best in Town," and the Cheesecake was really wonderful as well, so we went with his suggestions. Throw in a couple cups of Espresso and some Anisette too, and we were still in heaven.

Needless to say, our meal was fantastic. We loved it. We loved Gino's and would be back for more.

We went back to Gino's a couple weeks later. Joe loved the Pate Segrete and kept talking about it. He was back for more. We loved the menu we had the last time, and pretty much went with the same again. When we were eating the Segrete Pasta I identified the secret ingredients. They were butter and Parmigiano, mixed into Gino's basic tomato sauce. Just a little butter and the grated Parmigiano does the trick for a tasty sauce. The recipe is in the book, and don't worry, we didn't eat the same thing every time we went to Gino's. Over the years, we pretty much had every dish on the menu, from; the Minestrone and Pasta Fagoli, Mani-cotti, Lasagna, Spaghetti & Meatballs, Chicken Parmigiano, Veal Marsala and all. Specials too! We ate it all. "And loved every minute of it." Gino's, we miss you so! But great memories linger on.

SALADS

Salads are a big part of any Italian menu. Usually pretty basic; a Tossed Green Salad, Insalata Caprese, or the World Famous Caesar Salad. We don't go too in-depth here, but the little we give you is a lot. You won't need much more when it comes to Italian Salads than a tasty Caesar, or Tossed Salad Dressing with our Famous Creamy Italian.

Caeser Salads always made with Romaine Lettuce, but the Creamy Italian Dressing can go on any number of different lettuces, including; Romaine, Iceberg, Mesclum, Red Leaf, or some elegant Boston. We especially love when tomatoes are at the peak of the season and you make a tossed salad with; Tomatoes, Cucumber, and Boston or crisp Iceberg Lettuce, you'll have a salad that just can't be beat! Mangia!

SECRET DRESSING
- *CREAMY ITALIAN*

INGREDIENTS:

½ Cup Mayonnaise
¼ cup Olive Oil
¼ Red Wine Vinegar
1 tablespoon water
1 Garlic Clove, minced fine
¼ teaspoon each of Salt & Black Pepper
¼ teaspoon dry Oregano
¼ teaspoon dry Basil

Place Mayonnaise and half the Olive Oil in a mixing bowl and mix with a wire-whip. Add remaining Olive Oil, mix again.

Add vinegar a little at a time and mix.

Add all remaining ingredients and mix vigorously.

Place whatever lettuce you choose in a large bowl. Add Creamy Italian Dressing, mix and serve.

NOTE: You can make a salad with this tasty dressing with whatever lettuce and other ingredients you choose. Our favorite is Boston Bibb Lettuce with Cucumbers and Ripe Fresh Tomatoes. Iceberg or Romaine Lettuce also work well with the cucumbers and tomato, Buon Appetito and Enjoy!

CAESAR SALAD

Did you know that Caesar Salad is not really Italian? Well yes and no! The salad was created by an Italian, living in San Diego, California and working in Tijuana, Mexico. The salad that is said to be invented one day by Caesar Cardinini who was born in Italy and immigrated to the United States, settling in San Diego. I tis said that on the Fourth of July 1924, it was a very busy day with a large crowd of people at the restaurant and the place was running out of food stuffs. Cardini put together a few ingredients left in the house (the restaurant). The ingredients included; lettuce, Anchovies, eggs, bread (made in to croutons), capers, garlic, vinegar, and Parmesan Cheese. Cardini mixed then together and created the first-ever Caesar Salad. There have been many millions, maybe even into the billions of Caesar Salads served over the years. At first mostly in Italian Restaurants and Steak Houses, but nowadays in a number of restaurants, as long as they are not Asian or French, you might find a Caesar Salad. But mostly, most Americans (99%) see the Caesar Salad as Italian. I myself, thought for a number of years it was Mexican, as I thought it was invented in Tijuana, which it was, by a Mexican, which it was not. I finely found out it was invented by an Italian who immigrated to America, and this Italian Caesar Cardini invented the Caesar Salad in Tijuana Mexico.

Italian-American Cuisine as we've said before is a legitimate cuisine which is based on Italian Food from Italy with minor changes here-and-there do to local foods and the abundance or availability or not of certain foods. So the famed Caesar Salad invented by an Italian from Italy who was living in the United States but invented the first Caesar Salad in Mexico, "Yes The Caesar Salad is Italian-American," Basta!

CAESAR SALAD DRESSING

INGREDIENTS:

2 Cloves Garlic, peeled
5 Anchovy Filets, minced
2 large Egg Yolks
2 teaspoons Dijon Mustard
4 teaspoons fresh Lemon Juice
2 teaspoons Worcestershire Sauce
½ teaspoon ground Black Pepper
2/3 cup Olive Oil (not Extra Virgin as the taste is too strong) half cup grated Parmigiano Reggiano Cheese
1 large head Romaine Lettuce, chopped in large chunks or cut into 4 equal size wedges
½ cup store-bought or home-made croutons

Place all ingredients except the olive oil and cheese in a food processor with the blade attachment. Process for 1 minute until all ingredients are thoroughly incorporated.

Slowly add the olive oil little-by-little
as the processor is turn one.

Remove ingredients and place in a bowl.
Add grated half of the cheese and mix by hand.

If making your Caesar Salad with wedges, place a wedge on four separate plates, dress the lettuce wedges with the dressing and remaining cheese and top with Croutons. If using chopped lettuce, place the lettuce in a large bowl, add the dressing, toss the lettuce & dressing and mix until completely coated. Divide the dressed lettuce equally onto 4 plates, sprinkle with remaining cheese and croutons and serve.

NOTE: One very American thing to do, that's not Italian-American but created by Americans is *Grilled Chicken Caesar Salad*. It's quite popular and millions are sold every year in restaurants all over the country. To make Grilled Chicken Caesar Salad, simply grill boneless chicken breast, slice the breast and neatly arrange on top of a regular Caesar Salad, and Viola, you've got *Grilled Chicken Caesar Salad*, simple as that!

PASTA SALAD

Cold Pasta Salad was a dish that along with Pasta Primavera was all the rage back in the 70's. the popularity has waned a bit since then, but many people still love it, make it, and eat it. The dish is quick and easy to make, and if you put it on the table, everyone is sure to enjoy it.

This salad is a great item for a buffet table or Pot Luck Dinner. Mangia Bene!

INGREDIENTS:

1 pound Fusilli, or short pasta of your choice
2 Carrots, peeled and cut into ½ " cubes
1 – 10 ounce box of Frozen Peas
half pound Green Beans
8 spears of Asparagus, cut into 1 ½" pieces
half cup Green Olives with or without pimentos
15 – 20 Cherry Tomatoes cut in half
8 tablespoons Olive Oil
3 tablespoons Red Wine Vinegar
¼ cup Chives or Chopped Fresh Parsley
¼ teaspoon of Salt & ½ teaspoon Black Pepper

Cook pasta according to directions on package.

Break off ends of green beans and cut in half.

Place carrots into a pot with boiling salted water. Cook on a rapid boil for 3 minutes.

Add green beans with pot with carrots and cook for 2 minutes. Add Asparagus and cook for 3 minutes.

Drain the vegetables in a colander, then run cold water over vegetables to stop them from cooking.

Place back in colander, shaking the water off of the vegetables to get them as dry as possible.

Place the cooked pasta, all the vegetables, and all the remaining ingredients in a large glass or ceramic bowl and mix thoroughly. Let rest and marinate for a half hour or more, or the salad can be serve immediately.

GARLIC BREAD

Garlic Bread? You're not gonna find this in many cookbooks. Garlic Bread was once upon a time, in the heyday of Old School Italian Red-Sauce Joints a hugely popular standard staple of just about every Italian Restaurant of the day. It was mostly found in restaurants, but some families liked it so much, they might make it at home. My sister Barbara did, and she used to make it all the time. The recipe follows.

BAZZY'S GARLIC BREAD

1 Large Loaf Italian Bread
3 cloves Garlic, peeled and minced fine
2 tablespoons Olive Oil
2 tablespoons Butter, melted
¼ teaspoon ground Black Pepper
3 tablespoons grated Parmesan
1 teaspoon dry Oregano
3 tablespoons Fresh Parsley, chopped (optional)

Mix all ingredients together in a bowl.

Heat oven to 350 degrees.

Slice the loaf of bread in-half lengthwise. Spread Garlic-Butter mixture over each half loaf of bread.

Bake in oven for 10-12 minutes until bread just starts to get slightly browned. Cut into thick slices and serve immediately.

ANTIPASTI

Antipasti, or in the singular starts off an Italian Meal. Not always, but in principal, if you're in Italy, or if at a restaurant in America, you might get some sort of Antipasto to start off you meal. If in Tuscany, Crostini al Toscana is the # 1 choice, in Emilia Romagna it might be Prosciutto di Parma or Culatello, and in Napoli Vongole al Posillipo.

In an Italian-American Household you might get a favorite of Stuffed Artichokes or a tossed Green Salad. Many of our Sunday Meals would start with the famed Italian-American Antipasto Misto of Salami, Provolone, Celery Sticks, Sicilian Olives and Roast Peppers. In an Italian Restaurant in America you might have the same or very similar Mixed Antipasto and there will be a munch bigger selection of items. Things like; Stuffed Mushrooms, Stuffed Peppers, Hot Antipasto, Baked Clams Oreganata, and Fried Calamari.

In this section of Antipasto Recipes, we've include a few of our favorites along with a few surprises, like Buffalo Chicken Wings. Well you'll not find these baby's on any Italian Restaurant menu, but guess what? They are

Italian! Italian-American that is! And we've included them because they were created by Italian-Americans in Buffalo, and not for that reason, but because they are as tasty as can be, and because of that, have become a greater success then anyone could have ever imagined. They are an American favorite, Millions of these "little suckers" are eaten every day all across America, and even the World. They're Huge!

Some of our favorites (antipasto), and all Italian-Americans that we've include recipes here are; Clams Posillipo, Stuffed Mushrooms, Stuffed Peppers, Clams Casino, Shrimp Cocktail, and Arancini (Sicilian Rice Balls). We love all these dishes and know you'll love them too.

ARANCINI
"SICILIAN RICE BALLS"

INGREDIENTS:

1 cup Rice (long grain or short)
4 cups water (for Rice)
½ teaspoon Spanish Saffron
6 ounces ground beef
1/2 cup minced Onion
½ cup frozen Peas
3 tablespoons Olive Oil
¼ teaspoon Salt, ¼ teaspoon Black Pepper
1/3 cup Butter
5 tablespoons grated Parmigiano Reggiano
1 medium Egg, beaten

For Breading:

2 extra large Eggs, beaten
2 ½ cups plain Breadcrumbs
2 cups Vegetable Oil to fry rice balls in

PREPARATION:

Wash rice. Cook in 4 cups water with Saffron until tender. About 14 minutes. Turn heat off, drain rice.

Let rice cool for 4 minutes. Add butter to rice and mix. Add Parmigiano Cheese and mix. Set aside.

Place ground beef oil, garlic and onion in saucepan and brown on low heat for 6 minutes. Add onions and cook 6 minutes on very low heat. Season with Salt & Black Pepper to taste. Add Peas, cook 2 minutes low heat.

Add 1 beaten egg to rice and mix.

Shape rice into balls the size of a Spalding Rubber Ball. Put ground beef mixture inside the rice balls and cover whole and re-shape into balls.

Dip rice balls into lightly beaten egg, roll in bread crumbs and fry in hot olive oil until golden brown all over.

CLAMS CASINO

Clams Casino was created in 1917 at the Little Casino at Narragansett, Rhode Island and has been a huge hit ever since. This dish has been a favorite Italian-American Classics, mostly in restaurants. The dish was hugely popular in the 1970'2 and 80's but has cooled off on popularity in recent years. It's still quite popular, but not so much as in those peak years when it was on just about every single Italian Restaurant menu in America. Never the less, it's tasty as heck, and still has a great place in the Italian-American Culinary World.

Recipe:

24 Littleneck Clams (or Cherrystones)
6 Bacon Strips. Cook till lightly brown
½ pound Butter, soft at room temperature
1 small Red Bell Pepper, cleaned and diced fine
1 Green Bell Pepper, cleaned & diced fine
4 Garlic Cloves, peeled and minced fine
6 tablespoons Fresh chopped Parsley
Salt & Black Pepper
½ cup plain Bread Crumbs

Wash clams and place in a large pot with half a cup of water. Cover pot and turn on flame to high. Steam clams in covered pot just to the point that they have all opened. You need to mix the clams around in the pot with a wooden spoon while they are cooking. Cover pot after mixing.

As soon as all the clams are opened remove from heat and set aside to cool.

Dice 2 of the Bacon Strips fine and place in a mixing bowl with all remaining ingredients, except the breadcrumbs. Season to taste with salt & black pepper. Mix all ingredients into the softened butter with a wooden spoon.

After the clams have cooled, remove from pot and remove the top part of the calm shell while leaving the meat of the clam in the bottom half shell with any remaining juices from the clam (do not discard clam juice).

Cut bacon into little squares that will fit into the clam shells. Place about 1 tablespoon of the butter mixture over the top of each clam. Sprinkle on a little bread-crumbs over the butter. Place 1 piece of Bacon on top. Place all the clams on a cookie sheet and bake in a 425 degree oven for about 10 minutes.

CLAMS POSILLIPO

3 dozen Littleneck Clams or 3 lbs.
or Cockles or Manila Clams
1 ½ cups Tomato Sauce
½ teaspoon Red Pepper flakes
½ cup dry White Wine
7 cloves of garlic, peeled and sliced
1 ½ cups water
3 tablespoons fresh Parsley, roughly chopped
Olive Oil

Put wine into a large pot and turn flame on to high. Cook and reduce the wine to half its original volume.

Add water, garlic, Red Pepper, and tomato sauce. Bring to boil. Lower to a simmer and let cook three minutes.

Add Clams to pot. Turn heat up to high. Cover pot. Cook and watch when clams have opened. Once the clams have opened, lower heat to medium. Remove cover. Mix clams with a large spoon while cooking for 1 ½ minutes. Turn flame off. Add Parsley and mix. Portion out into pasta bowls, equal portions of Clams and broth for each person.

SHRIMP COCKTAIL

Shrimp Cocktail is a great favorite of just about all Italians, and all of America. Originally not really Italian, but Italian-Americans have adopted it into their cuisine. "Once Upon a Time" Shrimp Cocktail was on just about every Italian Restaurant Menu in America.

2 lbs. Large Shrimp, cleaned
1 tablespoon of Salt, ½ cup Tomato Ketchup
3 tablespoons Prepared Horseradish
8 drops Tabasco sauce or other Hot Sauce Brand

Bring a large pot of salted water to the boil.

Add shrimp. Bring back to the boil and once the water comes back to the boil, lower heat to lowest flame and cook for about 4-5 minutes until shrimp are cooked through and you do not see any rawness in the center.

Immediately remove from heat, and drain water off shrimp. Add shrimp to a large bowl of water with ice to stop the cooking. Let sit for 5 minutes. Drain the shrimp of all water and set to the side.

In a small glass or ceramic bowl, mix the horseradish. Ketchup and Hot Sauce. This is the

Cocktail Sauce for the shrimp. Neatly arrange shrimp on a plate or platter and serve with the cocktail sauce in a small bowl.

TUSCAN WINGS

These are tasty little Chicken Wings my Uncle Frank used to whip up every now and then. This is a great one pan dish, and is all you'll need for a nice tasty dinner. A Caesar Salad or Tossed Salad with Creamy Italian Dressing makes a tasty starter to proceed the Chicken Wings.

30 Chicken Wings
15 tablespoons olive oil
½ teaspoon each of Salt & Black Pepper
4 Sprigs Fresh Rosemary, broken in half
10 cloves Garlic, peeled and cut in half
4 Idaho Potatoes, peeled and cut into large chunks, about 10 pieces per potato
1 teaspoon Dry Oregano

Place the chicken wings in a large pan that you will be roasting them in. Add 10 tablespoons of olive oil, Salt & Pepper and mix.

Place potatoes in a pot of boiling salted water. Cook potatoes for 3 minutes. Remove from heat, drain the potatoes and set aside.
Roast the chicken in a 400 degree oven for 15 minutes.

Add potatoes, rosemary, garlic, and remaining olive oil to pan, and mix.

Roast at 350 degrees for 10 to 12 minutes, until chicken is fully cooked.

Remove from oven and let chicken rest for 6 minutes.

Add Oregano to pan and mix thoroughly.

Serve and enjoy.

NOTE: You can make this dish, with or without the potatoes. Make the potatoes if you're having this for a main-course. If just making as appetizers, make without the potatoes.

STUFFED MUSHROOMS

Once Upon a Time Stuffed Mushrooms were on each and every Italian Restaurant menu in the country. Well, at least 90 % anyway. Yes, they were. And I'm talking about the 60's, 1970's, and into the 80's mostly. You don't find them as much these days, but they're still great and most Italian-Americans love em. In old school Italian Red Sauce Restaurants back in the day, they'd stand alone on their own as an antipasto item, or they'd be included in the once popular Hot Antipasto, along with a Baked Clam, Stuffed Peppers, and Eggplant Rolatina. "Oh the good old days!" This is my Grandmothers recipe below. Make them at home for an antipasto, serve them at a party on the buffet table or bring them to a pot luck dinner. They're sure to please.

24 medium sized domestic Button Mushrooms
1 small Onion, peeled and minced
6 tablespoons Olive Oil, Tbs. butter
¼ cup Italian-Style Breadcrumbs
¼ cup grated Parmigiano Reggiano Cheese
Salt & Pepper to taste
¼ cup fresh chopped Italian Parsley
Brush off and remove any dirt that might be on the mushrooms and clean well. Break off

mushroom stems and chop fine. Place Olive Oil, butter, onions, and chopped mushroom stems in a large frying pan and cook over low heat for about 7 minutes until mushrooms and onions are cooked through. Set aside and let cool.

Add the breadcrumbs to pan with the cooled mushrooms and mix. Add all remaining ingredients and mix well. The mixture should be just slightly moist. If its not, you can add a little bit more olive oil or a little water just to moisten the mixture a little.

Fill each Mushroom Cap with the breadcrumb mushroom mixture so there is a little heaping dome on the each mushroom cap.

Heat the oven to 375 degrees. Place all the mushrooms in a baking pan with a thin film of olive oil on bottom of pan. Bake mushrooms for about 15 minutes until the mushrooms are cooked through. Serve and enjoy.

BUFFALO WINGS
ORIGINAL RECIPE
"YES THEY'RE ITALIAN"
Italian-American

After Burgers and Pizza, these Buffalo Chicken Wings may very well be America's 3rd most popular dish. And guess what? They're not just American, they're Italian American Teressa Bellissimo one night at her families Anchor Bar in Buffalo New York. Legend has it that Teressa's son Dom was hanging out at the bar one night with his buddy's. The guys were hungry so Mamma Bellissimo whipped up a little snack for the boys. Teressa fried up some wings, made a little hot sauce and coated the wings with them. And served them to the boys. They went nuts they loved them. They started serving them as a free at the bar for the bar customers. It was just a matter of weeks before all of Buffalo found out about these tasty wings. They became famous almost over night, whereby the Bellissimo's stopped serving them for free at the bar and put them on the menu. The Bellissimo's served Italian Food at their Anchor Bar, and the Italian Food was quite special. However the Bellisimo's tasty Chicken Wings quickly out sold all the regular Italian Specialty Dishes and the Bellissimo's Wings became the number 1 best seller on the menu. Not only that, but Teressa's Italian-American created Chicken Wings became uber famous all over America and subsequently all over the World. That's Italian, "Italian-American."

Ingredients:

36 chicken wing pieces
(one wing makes 2 pieces - the "flat"
& the drum)
1 tablespoon vegetable oil, 1/2 teaspoon salt
1 cup all-purpose flour
1 1/2 tablespoons white vinegar
1/4 teaspoon cayenne pepper
1/8 teaspoon garlic powder
1/4 teaspoon Worcestershire sauce
1 teaspoon Tabasco sauce
6 tablespoons Frank's Hot Sauce (or other)
6 tablespoons unsalted Butter or Margarine
Celery Sticks
1 bottle of Blue Cheese Dressing

Preheat oven to 425 degrees F. Cut whole wings into two pieces at the joint. In a bowl toss the wings with the oil, and salt. Place into a large plastic shopping bag, and add the flour.

Shake to coat evenly. Remove wings from the bag, shaking off excess flour, and spread out evenly on oiled foil-lined baking pan(s). Do not crowd. Bake for about 20 minutes, turn the wings over, and cook another 20 minutes, or until the wings are cooked through and browned.

While the Wings are baking, mix all the ingredients for the sauce in a pan and cook over low heat for 6 minutes, stirring occasionally.

After the Wings are cooked, remove from oven. Place Wings in a large bowl and pour sauce over the wings to coat. Mix thoroughly. Serve with Blue Cheese Dressing and fresh Celery Spears.

LUCIA'S STUFFED PEPPERS

These Stuffed Peppers where one of the favorite dishes in my mother Lucia Bellino's repertoire of tasty Italian-American dishes. We always had them as a main course, but you can serve them as an antipasto item. Serve one for an antipasto, or 2 for a main-course. And always Bon Appetito!

Ingredients:

1 medium onion, minced
3 cloves of garlic, minced
6 Tablespoons chopped parsley
6 Tablespoons bread crumbs
2 eggs. Salt & pepper
1 cup long grain rice
¾ lb. ground pork
¾ lb. ground beef
1 Tablespoon Dry Oregano
½ cup grated Pecorino Romano
4 Red or Green bell peppers
½ cup chicken broth
1-1/2 cups tomato sauce

Preparation for Lucia's Stuffed Peppers:

Cook the rice for 12 minutes in boiling water and drain.

Cut the tops off the peppers and reserve.

Mix all remaining ingredients except the Broth and sauce in a large bowl.

Stuff the peppers with the meat mixture and top with the Pepper tops.

Place the peppers in a small baking pan with the broth. Cover with aluminum foil. Bake at 350 for 40 minutes. Remove foil and continue Baking for 15 minutes longer.

Heat the tomato sauce.

Put 6 Tbs. of sauce on a plate with a pepper.

Serve with grated cheese.

ZUPPA

Zuppa? Soup? What to say? Well, a whole lot. Soup is one of the great wonders of culinary delights. One of the easiest items in the culinary world to prepare. Soup is very forgiving, in both it's cooking, storing and re-heating. Soup, like stew heat so very well and do not suffer from doing so. Once a steak is made, you can't really heat it, you've got to eat it right then and there. Not so with soup. Soup is great any old time of the day; for lunch, dinner, even breakfast and any time in-between. When you have made a pot of soup, you eat some after you've made it, then store the rest for a number of quick and easy meals to come.

My, mom used to make us good hearty soup all the time, and we especially loved so good hot steam soup on a cold winters day. Mommy used to make us; Split Pea, Beef Barley, Minestrone, and Pasta Fagoli. We loved her Minestrone which she got a really good recipe from Father Dominic. We've include it here, along with Pasta Fazool, Zuppa di Aglio (Garlic Soup), and the famed soup of Uncle Pete.

It's one we know most of you have probably never had, it's Uncle Pete's Spare Rib Soup, and it's amazing. We're sure you'll agree. Make it, and watch your friends will go nuts.

FATHER DOMENIC'S MINESTRONE

INGREDIENTS:

8 tablespoons Olive Oil
8 cloves of Garlic, peeled and minced fine
2 large Onions, peeled and chopped
½ teaspoon Red Pepper Flakes
3 stalks of Celery, washed and sliced
1 – 16 oz. can whole Plum Tomatoes
¼ cup fresh Basil, 1 Bay Leaf
4 Carrots, peeled and sliced
2 Idaho Potatoes, peeled and cut to 1 1/2 " cubes
3 Zucchini, washed and sliced thick
1 – 14 oz. can Cannellini Beans, drain and washed
1 - 10 ounce pack Frozen Peas
10 cups water
1 teaspoon Sea Salt, 1 teaspoon Black Pepper

Place Olive Oil and Onions in a large non corrosive-pot. Turn on heat to medium flame and cook for 6 minutes. Add Garlic and Red Pepper and cook for 4 minutes.

Add tomatoes and turn heat to high. Cook for 3 minutes on high heat while stirring constantly. Add Basil, cook for 1 minute.

Add water and carrots and bring to the boil. Cook for 4 minutes at a rapid boil.

Add potatoes and cook at a rapid boil for 5 minutes.

Add Zucchini and lower heat. Cook for 15 minute at a low simmer. Add beans and continue cooking on low flame for 8 minutes.

Add frozen Peas and cook for 3 minutes. Your Minestrone is ready to serve. Serve with Olive Oil and Grated Parmigiano Reggiano Cheese on the side.

JOHNNY GOOMBA'S PASTA FAZOOL

This Johnny Goomba's secret recipe for Pasta Faazool, a.k.a. "Pasta Fagoli" that Johnny gave to us one day. Guess it's not a *Secret* any more? Enjoy!

2 medium onions, 3 celery stalks, chopped
2 carrots, minced
½ lb. pancetta, minced finely. ¼ cup olive oil
8 cloves garlic, peeled and cut into thirds
1 lb. dried cannellini beans,
soaked in water overnight
2 sprigs fresh rosemary. 1 bay leaf
1 ½ cups canned plum tomatoes
4 cups chicken broth
4 cups water. Salt & pepper to taste
1 lb. Ditalini
Preparation:

Sauté pancetta in a large pot for 3 minutes. Add garlic & onions. Sauté for 6 minutes on low heat.

Add celery and carrots. Sauté for 4 minutes.

Add tomatoes, beans, broth, & water. Bring up to the boil, then lower to a slow simmer and cook for 1 ½ hours until the beans are tender.

Remove half the beans and mash through a food mill or puree in a blender.

Place the mashed beans back into the pot with the whole beans.

Put remainder of olive oil in a pan with 6 cloves of garlic, a bay leaf, and rosemary. Cook over medium heat for 6 minutes. This is called a perfume.

Strain the perfume into the pot of soup, mix and simmer the soup with perfume for 12 minutes.

Cook the ditalini according to instructions on.

To serve, put ½ cup cooked ditalini in a soup bowl. Fill the bowl with the bean soup. Sprinkle a little Extra-virgin olive oil over the soup. Pass around Parmigiano and enjoy.

UNCLE PETE'S SPARE RIB SOUP

You're gonna love this one! If you don't something is wrong with you. It's Uncle Pete's Spare Ribs & Bean Soup. Wow. If you love Ribs like we do, you'll go nits for this tasty and quite hearty soup from our Uncle Pete. There's nothing like it on a cold Winters Day. But it's not just for winter. It's easy to make, and so dam tasty you'll want to eat it all the time.

INGREDIENTS:

3 pounds Pork Spare Ribs
1 pound Dry Cranberry Beans, soaked in water over night
5 ½ quarts of water
7 tablespoons Olive Oil
2 medium Onions, peeled and chopped
6 Garlic Cloves, peeled and sliced
1 teaspoon Red Pepper Flakes
4 Carrots, peeled and sliced thick
1 – 28 can whole Plum Tomatoes
1 bay leaf, Salt & Black Pepper
3 large Idaho Potatoes, peeled and sliced thick
½ pound Ditalini Pasta

Place Olive Oil and Onions in a large pot and cook on low heat for 6 minutes. Add Garlic and Red-Pepper flakes and continue cooking three minutes.

Add tomatoes, turn heat to high and cook five minutes while stirring.

Add water, Beans, and Pork Ribs, and bring to the boil. Once all has come to the boil, add Bay Leaf, turn the heat down to the simmer and cook on low heat for one hour.

After the soup has been simmering for 1 hour, add the carrots. Simmer another hour on low heat, then add the potatoes.

Cook the Ditalini according to direction on package, drain, then set aside until later.

Continue cooking for about 45 minutes, until the ribs are cooked and tender. Total cooking time is about 2 hours and 45 minutes. The soup is ready to serve.

Place a half cup of cooked Ditalini in a bowl and top with soup. Make sure everyone gets their fare-share of ribs. Eat it, and enjoy.

ZUPPA di AGLIO "Garlic Soup"

¼ cup Olive Oil, ¼ cup Butter
½ loaf Italian Bread cut in to 2 " cubes
½ loaf Italian Bread cut into ½ inch slices
24 Cloves of Garlic, peeled
¼ cup fresh chopped Italian Parsley
2 heads of Garlic, left whole and un-peeled
1 large Onion, sliced
2 Carrots, peeled and sliced
¼ cup Red Wine
7 cups Chicken Broth, 2 cups water
2 Bay Leaves
Salt & Black Pepper

Place Olive Oil, Butter, and peeled Garlic in a large pot. Cook over low heat for 4 minutes. Add bread and cook for 7 minutes at medium temperature until bread is nicely browned, being careful not to burn. Remove bread from pot and set aside.

Add Onions and Parsley and cook on medium heat for 7 minutes. Add wine and cook on high heat for 4 minutes.

Add chicken broth, whole heads of Garlic, carrots, Bay Leaves, and water. Bring to the boil. Once the broth has come to the boil, low heat so the soup is cooking at a medium simmer for 20 minutes.

While the soup is simmering, toast the slices of Italian Bread. Then rub each piece of the toasted bread with a clove of peeled garlic. Set the bread aside.

Put cubed bread in pot with soup and cook for 6 minutes.

Take 3 cups of the broth from the large pot and put in a small pot where you will cook the eggs in the broth. Bring this to a low simmer.

Place 4 eggs in the small pot with just the broth and poach at low heat for 3 minutes. Turn off.

Discard the whole heads of garlic from the soup. Ladle soup with garlic cloves and cubed bread and onions into 4 soup bowls.

Add 1 poached egg into each soup bowl. Place two slices of toasted bread in each soup bowl and top with grated Parmigiano Cheese. Drizzle some Olive Oil on top of each soup and serve.

Note: Take the broth that you cooked the eggs in and put back in the pot with the rest of the soup. Let cool, then put in containers, cover tightly, and store in refrigerator for another days meal.

CECI BEAN SOUP

1 pound dry Chick Peas,
soaked overnight in water
1/4 cup Italian Olive Oil
1 medium Onion, peeled and minced
2 Celery stalks, washed and chopped fine
1 Carrot, peeled and minced
1 Baking Potato, cut in ½ " cubes
6 garlic cloves, peeled and minced fine
6 San Marzano Plum Tomatoes
1 teaspoon dry Sage
Salt & Black Pepper
1 pound Imported Italian Ditalini
(or Ronzoni)

Place olive oil, onion and celery in a large non-corrosive pot. Cook over low heat for 7 minutes.

Add garlic and cook on low heat for 3 minutes. Add tomatoes, turn heat to high and cook for 4 minutes. Add celery, cook 1 minute. Add water and dry ceci beans.
Bring water to the boil. Once water comes to boil, lower heat to low simmer. Add potatoes.

Cook on a low simmer for about 1 hour and a half or 1 hour 45 minutes until the Ceci Beans are soft, yet slightly firm. Add sage in last 20 minutes of cooking at which time you should cook the pasta. Remove 1 ½ cups of the Ceci Beans and puree. Add back to soup, mix and cook 5 minutes.

Cook Pasta according to directions on package. Drain pasta, reserving 1 cup water to put into the soup. Add pasta to the soup, cook five minutes.

Serve with grated Pecorino Romano Cheese. Put the leftover soup in containers in the refrigerator to enjoy later on in the week.

Soups like Pasta Ceci, Pasta & Peas, Zuppe di Lentiche and Pasta Fagoli were all very popular with Italian Immigrants in the early 1900's and onwards. As most Italian families were on limited incomes and these soups were one of the cheapest things they could make. Cheap, but good, and oh so healthy. They carry on with many Italian Americans to this very day, whether wealthy, poor, or anywhere in-between, we all love these hearty Italian Soups.

PASTA
a.k.a. "MACCHERONI

Pasta, who amongst us doesn't love it? Nobody! Pasta, "some call it Maccheroni." We do. We love it! Can't get enough of it. Have to have it practically each-and-every-day. Just About. Pasta is the cornerstone of the Italian Diet, and we just can't live without it, whether it's Linguine with Clam Sauce, Spaghetti & Meatballs, Fettuccine Bolognese, Gnocchi, Bucatini Amatriciana, Raviolis, or whatever pasta it may be, we just can't get enough.

I always like to tell a couple stories of my Cousin Joe, who was the greatest pasta lover I've ever known. Joe had to have pasta every day. He couldn't live without it. One Sunday afternoon we were hanging out and we would be going to Joe's father's house for dinner. Joe's dad was making Salmon and Lobsters for dinner, but know pasta. We were going to leave for Uncle Joe's house in less than an hour. Joe was dying for some pasta, and he knew his father wasn't going to be making any. Cousin Joe timidly asked me (he was almost embarrassed) if I could quick whip up some Spaghetti Pomodoro for him? I knew he was suffering, so I said yes of course. He always does things for me. I grabbed some garlic, olive oil, and a couple cans of San Marzano and got a quick Pomodoro going. I let it cook about 10 minutes when I dropped the pasta in the boiling water. The sauce would cook another 10 minutes as the spaghetti was cooking. Ten minutes later, I drained the spaghetti, then threw it back in the pot, sprinkled on a little olive oil, mixed it up, then threw in some of the sauce and mixed. I put some Spaghetti on a plate for Joe and one for me, then topped with a little more tomato sauce each and sprinkled on a little olive oil. We sat down, grated a hunk of Parmigiano over each of our pasta plates, and we were in Heaven. Especially Joe. Just 25 minutes from start eating the Spaghetti. That's the power of Pasta! Some call it Maccheroni

GRANDMA'S TOMATO SAUCE

There are a number of different versions of Tomato Sauce, know as either Salsa Pomodoro or Sugo di Pomodoro in Italy, and as Tomato Sauce or simply Sauce in the Italian-American community. This recipe is for Tomato Sauce in its simplest form, using Olive Oil that's flavored with Garlic and Pepperoncino (Red Pepper Flakes) to season the oil which seasons the tomatoes along with fresh Basil (Basilico). Many Italian-Americans and most Americans not of Italian ancestry like and think that Oregano is a standard and must have ingredient in Tomato Sauce. It is not, but if you like it go right ahead and put it in. In Italy, you rarely see Oregano in Sugo di Pomodoro, and this is how the recipe here is. The recipe for Marinara has Oregano in the recipe. The two recipes are similar, but do have differences in that the Marinara has tomato paste and parsley and this recipe does not. Make them both and decide which you like better. They're both great.

INGREDIENTS:

3-28 oz. cans San Marzano crushed tomatoes
or other good quality Italian style tomatoes
7 cloves minced garlic
1 small onion, minced
½ teaspoon crushed red pepper
¼ cup virgin olive oil
¼ cup chopped fresh basil or 1 tsp. dried
Salt and pepper to taste

In a 6 quart or larger pot, sauté onions over a low flame for 3 minutes. Add garlic and cook for 3-4 minutes. Do not let the garlic get dark or burn.

Add tomatoes, turn heat up to high and stir. When sauce starts to bubble, turn flame down so the sauce is at a low simmer. Simmer for 45 minutes while frequently stirring the bottom of the pan to keep sauce from burning. Add fresh basil in the last ten minutes of cooking.

Cook whatever pasta you choose (spaghetti is best) according to directions on package. Drain pasta, toss with tomato sauce and a drizzle of olive oil, plate, and serve with cheese.

MARINARA SAUCE

Recipe:

10 tablespoons Olive Oil
8 Garlic Cloves
16 Sprigs Fresh Italian Parsley
3/4 teaspoon Black Pepper, ½ teaspoon Salt,
1 teaspoon Oregano
2 – 28 cans Tomato
2 tablespoons Tomato Paste

Place Olive Oil and Garlic in a medium size non-corrosive pot. Cook on low heat for 5 minutes.

Add chopped Parsley, salt, pepper, and Oregano, and cook on low heat for 2 minutes.

Add tomatoes. Cook on high heat for 3 minutes while stirring constantly with a wooden spoon.

Lower flame to low heat and cook for 35 minutes, stirring occasionally so does not stick or burn.

Serve with any pasta you like; Spaghetti, Raviolis, Rigatoni, etc.. Basta!

GINO'S SECRET SAUCE
"SALSA SEGRETE"

Salsa Segrete. This was the most famous dishes at on of New York's most popular old-school Italian Red-Sauce Joints for years. The restaurant in question was none other than Gino's of Lexington Avenue, across the street from Bloomingdale's. Gino's was a wond-erful little restaurant that had a long standing well-healed clientele of loyal regulars, that included the likes of one Frank Sinatra, along with Joe DiMaggio, Tony Bennett, Gay Talese and too many to name here.

Gino's was a classic old-school Italian favorite that had all the usual suspects of Red Sauce Joints of yesteryear. Dishes like; Spaghetti & Meatballs, Baked Clams, Shrimp Scampi, Chicken Parmigiano and all the rest. Gino's served these great dishes at very reasonable prices, with nice friendly service and a warm wonderful atmosphere. The dining room walls were lined with their famous (and infamous) Scalamandre Zebra Wall Paper. Equally as famous as Gino's Zebra Wall Paper was the Dish Rigatoni with Salsa Segrete, Secret Sauce. It was a uber tasty pasta of a tomato sauce with secret ingredients that the owner refused to divulge the recipe of. Well, we got our hands on it a couple years ago, and though Gino's sadly closed its doors in 2011, you can with secret recipe make Gino's famed Rigatoni with Salsa Segrete. "All you need is some Zebra Wall Paper," to relive the memories of our beloved and sorely missed Gino's.

Yes, Gino's was a great restaurant, loved by its many regulars, who included the likes of; Frank Sinatra, Gay Talese, "Joltin" Joe DiMaggio, Ed Sullivan, and Woody Allen, just to name a few.

There were many favorite dishes at Gino's, but one favorite was the most famous dish of all. Most famous at Gino's that is. The dish was Rigatoni con Salsa Segreto. Rigatoni with Secret Sauce.

"The SECRET SAUCE"
THE SECRET RECIPE! Ssshhhhhhs !!!

The Ingredients: "That's The SECRET"

1-28 oz. cans San Marzano crushed tomatoes or other good quality Italian style tomatoes2 cloves minced garlic1 small onion, minced 1/8 teaspoon crushed red pepper
5 tablespoons cup virgin olive oil
¼ cup chopped fresh basil
or 1 teaspoon dried
Salt and pepper to taste
½ tablespoon Butter
½ cup grated Parmigiano Reggiano Cheese

Make Tomato Sauce (recip3 precedes)

In a 6 quart or larger pot, sauté onions over a low flame for 3 minutes. Add garlic and cook for 3-4 minutes. Do not let the garlic get dark or burn.

Add tomatoes, turn heat up to high and stir. When sauce starts to bubble, turn flame down so the sauce is at a low simmer.

Simmer for 45 minutes while frequently stirring the bottom of the pan to keep sauce from burning. Add fresh basil in at the last ten minutes of cooking.

Cook whatever pasta you choose (spaghetti is best) according to directions on package. Drain pasta, toss with tomato sauce and a drizzle of olive oil, plate, and serve with Cheese.

Cook a pound of Pasta of your choice for 4 people, if just 2 people than cook a half pound of pasta, and cut the amount of Butter and Grated Parmigiano Cheese by half. Cook pasta according to directions on package. If using fresh Tagliolini or Fettuccine, the pasta will be cooked in 3-4 minutes.

Drain the pasta. Add to tomato sauce. Turn off heat. Add Butter and mix. Add grated cheese and mix. Serve the Pasta. Pass more grated Parmigiano to top the pasta with, eat and enjoy, "I guarantee you will."

SPAGHETTI PUTTANESCA
alla GISELLA

This is the fame pasta dish of Napoli says made by Neopolitan Ladies of the Night (Prostitutes) to lure prospective clients with its heady-aroma. Another version is that, it's tasty and quick to prepare, and the ladies could quickly make it in-between customers. Whatever the true story, the pasta is ultra tasty and popular as can be. This is the Secret Recipe of one of the famed ladies called Gisella.

INGREDIENTS:

10 tablespoons Olive Oil
6 Garlic Cloves, peeled and sliced thin
½ cup Gaeta or other small Black Olives
¼ cup Sicilian Capers (or other)
6 Anchovy Filets, minced fine
1 teaspoon Red Pepper Flakes
2 ½ cups Tomato Sauce from recipe in book
1 pound imported Italian Spaghetti

Place Olive Oil and Garlic in a large frying pan. Turn heat on to medium and cook 2 minutes. Add Anchovies and cook 3 minutes on a low flame.

Add Red Pepper, Olives, and Capers and cook on low flame for 3 minutes. Add tomato sauce and cook on low heat for 10 minutes. While the sauce is cooking, place spaghetti in a large pot of rapidly boiling salted water. Cook spaghetti according to directions on package.

When spaghetti is done cooking, drain in a colander and reserve 10 tablespoons of the pasta cooking water.

Add spaghetti back to the pot it cooked in with the reserved cooking water. Sprinkle a little olive oil of pasta and mix.

Place have of the Puttanesca Sauce in the pot with the spaghetti and mix well. Plate the Spaghetti & Sauce evenly on to 4 plates or pasta bowls. Top each plate of spaghetti with ¼ portion of remaining sauce. Serve to guest, pretend you're in Bella Napoli and Enjoy!

FETTUCCINE ALFREDO
"The Recipe"

1 lb. fresh Fettuccine
1 pt. heavy cream, ½ stick butter
1 cup grated Parmigianno
2 egg yolks, salt & pepper

Put the cream in a large frying pan. Bring to the boil, lower the flame and let the cream cook. Season the cream with salt and pepper to taste. Reduce volume by One-Third, This will thicken the sauce.

Cook the fettuccine and drain it. Put the fettuccine in to the pan with the cream. Add butter and stir.

Turn the flame off. Add egg yolks and Parmigiano and stir. Serve and pass around extra Parmigiano.

Note: You can make *Fettuccine Lemone* by adding the zest of two lemons to this recipe. Fresh basil is also another nice addition for the Lemone Sauce. *Once Upon a Time* I was quite famous for this tasty *Sauce.*

Le CIRQUE'S PASTA PRIMAVERA

Pasta Primavera was another one of those 70's dishes that was all the rage at the time and into the 80's as well. The dish was created one day by renowned New York Restaurateur (from Italy), Mr. Siro Maccioni. The dish, was hugely popular at Sirio's uber hot Le Cirque's Restaurant, that at the time was the hottest most renowned restaurant for the Rich & Famous Celebrity and moneyed crowd. For years, this dish that was the signature dish of the restaurant and made "World Famous," was not on the menu, and you could only get it, if you were "In The Know." It was always available, all you had to do was ask for it, but it was not publicized, "a little Secret" of Sirio's so-to-speak. And here you have it! The Original Recipe of Sirio Maccioni's Pasta Primavera.

SPAGHETTI PRIMAVERA
"Original Recipe"

INGREDIENTS:

1 bunch Broccoli
4 Asparagus Spears, 2 small Zucchini
1/2 cup fresh or frozen peas
1 ½ cups Green Bean
1/2 cup fresh or frozen peas
3/4 cup fresh or frozen pea pods
1 tablespoon peanut, vegetable or corn oil
2 cups thinly sliced mushrooms
Freshly ground black pepper
1/4 teaspoon dried Red-Pepper Flakes
1/4 cup finely chopped parsley
6 tablespoons olive oil
1 teaspoon minced garlic
3 cups 1-inch tomato cubes
6 basil leaves, chopped
1 pound spaghetti
4 tablespoons butter
2 tablespoons chicken broth
1/2 cup heavy cream, approximately
1/2 cup grated Parmesan
1/3 cup toasted pine nuts

PREPARATION:

Trim broccoli and break into florets. Trim off ends of the zucchini. Cut into quarters, then cut into 1-inch or slightly longer lengths (about 1 1/2 cups). Cut each asparagus into 2-inch pieces. Trim beans and cut into 1-inch pieces.

Cook each of the green vegetables separately in boiling salted water to cover until crisp but tender. Drain well, then run under cold water to chill, and drain again thoroughly. Combine the cooked vegetables in a bowl.

Cook the peas and pods; about 1 minute if fresh; 30 seconds if frozen. Drain, chill with cold water and drain again. Combine with the vegetables.

In a skillet over medium-high heat, heat the peanut oil and add the mushrooms. Season to taste. Cook about 2 minutes, shaking the skillet and stirring. Add the mushrooms, chili and parsley to the vegetables.

Heat 3 tablespoons olive oil in a saucepan and add half the garlic, tomatoes, salt and pepper. Cook about 4 minutes. Add the basil.

Heat 3 tablespoons olive oil in a large skillet and add the remaining garlic and the vegetable mixture. Cook, stirring gently, until heated through.

Cook the spaghetti in boiling salted water until almost (but not quite) tender, retaining a slight resilience in the center. Drain well.

In a pot large enough to hold the spaghetti and vegetables, add the butter and melt over medium-low heat. Then add the chicken broth and half a cup each of cream and cheese, stirring constantly. Cook gently until smooth. Add the spaghetti and toss quickly to blend. Add half the vegetables and pour in the liquid from the tomatoes, tossing over very low heat.

Add the remaining vegetables. If the sauce seems dry, add 3 to 4 tablespoons more cream. Add the pine nuts and give the mixture a final tossing.

Serve equal portions of the spaghetti mixture in hot soup or spaghetti bowls. Spoon equal amounts of the tomatoes over each serving. Serve immediately. Serves four.

JOEY CLAMS CLAM SAUCE
"Spaghetti w/ White Clam Sauce"

This is my good buddy "Joey Clams" recipe for Spaghetti al Vongole, a.k.a. Spaghetti with White Clam Sauce. This is how it's pretty much made in Italy. They don't normally make Red Clam Sauce in Italy. The tomato sauce is too over-powering and takes away from the taste of the clams, which as Robert DeNiro said as Jake LaMotta in Martin Scorsese's great film Raging Bull, "It defeats its own purpose." Fuhgetta-bout-It! If you want to make Spaghetti or Linguine with Red Clam Sauce go right ahead, use a lot or a little tomato sauce added to the recipe below. Less is much better, just to coat the pasta sort of, and you'll still be able to taste the clams.

Joey Clams recipe is great. He loves the dish and eats it all the time. Spaghetti or Linguine Vongole is one of the favorite and most loved of all Italian dishes in the Italian-American community. "We absolutely adore our Clam Sauce." Making Joe Clams Clam Sauce with this recipe and you will too. Buon Appetito!

INDGREDIENTS:

1 lb. top quality Imported Italian Spaghetti
(or Linguine)
1 lb. Cockles or Manila Clams
18 Littleneck Clams
¼ cup Olive Oil
4 cloves Garlic, peeled. Cut 3 cloves into thin slivers, keep one garlic clove whole.
1/8 teaspoon Red Pepper Flakes
Salt & Black Pepper
3 tablespoons chopped fresh Parsley (do not substitute dry Parsley) If you don't have fresh, don't use anything.
¼ cup Water

Place Littleneck clams in a medium size pot with a lid. Add Water and clams with 1 whole garlic clove, cover pot. Turn heat up to high and cook clams until they just open. Turn flame off. Remove clams from pot and reserve the cooking liquid.

Put a large pot of water on stove and bring to boil for cooking the pasta. Add Spaghetti or Linguine to pot of rapidly boiling water with salt and cook according to directions on package.

Sauté Garlic in Olive Oil in a large sauté pan over medium until garlic just starts to brown, lower heat to low and add Red Pepper. Cook 1 Minute. Turn off heat.

Add Cockles (or Manila Clams) to pan with garlic and olive oil. Add cooking liquid from larger Cherry Stone Clams to pan. Put cover on pan and turn heat to high, and cook until the Cockles (clams) just open.

Remove cooked Cherrystones from shells and chop each clam into about 6 pieces or so. Add the Chopped Cherrystone Clams to pan with Cockles.

When pasta is done cooking, drain it and add to pan with clams. Using a pair of tongs, mix pasta with clams, and cooking liquid.

Divide Pasta into 4 to 6 equal portions on a plate or pasta bowl. Divide all cooking liquid and Clams over each portion of Pasta on the plates. Sprinkle on some more Olive Oil once Pasta is plated. Enjoy.

Note: Do Not Put any Cheese over this Pasta. It's not recommended, but if you really must, then go ahead. "To each his own." But we strongly suggest you don't. Also, it is recommended you use either top quality Imported Italian Spaghetti or Linguine to make this dish the best it can taste. Do not use Fresh Pasta which I've seen people Sacrilegiously do on occasion. It doesn't go with the Clam Sauce, but then again, if you must you must. Serves 6-8 as part of 7 Fish Feast or 4 as a normal main course of a standard meal.

87

JERSEY SHORE CRAB SAUCE

There are plenty of Maryland Blue Crabs down on the Jersey Shore, as well as plenty of Italian-Americans. The two go together, and this Crab Sauce for pasta is a specialty of Jersey Italians who love seafood, along with their Brooklyn and New York neighbors. They all love it! So will you.

12 Hard Shell Blue Crabs
12 tablespoons Olive Oil
12 Cloves Garlic, 1 for each Crab,
peeled and chopped
1 Small Onion, peeled and chopped fine
1 teaspoon Red Pepper Flakes
1 – 28 oz. can whole San Marzano Tomatoes
1 – 28 oz. can Crushed Tomatoes
1 16 oz. can Tomato Puree
½ teaspoon dry Basil
¼ cup chopped fresh Italian Parsley
1 pound Lump Crab-Meat,
fresh frozen or canned
1 lb. imported Italian Spaghetti or Linguine

Put olive oil in a large pot and heat to high. Place the Crabs in the pot and sauté at high heat for 10 minutes.

After browning the crabs, remove from pan and set aside.
Put onions in pan and cook on medium heat for 5 minutes.

Add the garlic and red pepper to pan and cook on low heat for 3 minutes. Add whole tomatoes to pan and cook on high heat for 4 minutes whole stirring with a wooden spoon. Add crushed tomatoes and tomato puree. Add the Crabs back to the pot. Cook for 45 minutes on low heat.

Remove the crabs from pan and let cool on the side. Remove all the meat from the crabs and discard the shells. Add crab-meat to sauce with your extra pound of lump crab-meat.

Cook pasta according to directions on package. Drain pasta and put back in the pot it cooked in with 8 tablespoons of reserved pasta cooking water. Sprinkle pasta with a little olive oil and mix. Add 2 cups of crab sauce and half the parsley to pasta and mix.
Plate the pasta with sauce on 4 plates in equal portions and top with some more sauce and some parsley.

Notes: Do not serve with cheese! Italians never have cheese with Seafood Pasta. This is enough sauce for 2 to 3 pound of pasta, or about 12 portions, so after you make this Pasta with Crab Sauce with 1 pound of pasta, you still have plenty left over for another day.

RIGATONI all CONTADINA

Rigatoni Contadina is a great pasta dish (Sicilian) for those who love meat sauce, but don't want to make one (ragu) that takes so long as Bolognese, "The King of Italian Ragu." This meat ragu from Sicily is quite taste, but a little subtler than Bolognese. Bolognese having a fare amount of wine is richer. This meat ragu is tasty quick and easy to make.

1 pound imported Italian Rigatoni
6 links of Italian Sweet Sausage
1 small onion, peeled and minced
1 clove Garlic, peeled and minced fine
1 - 28 ounce can Crushed Tomato or Italian Passata di Pomodoro
4 tablespoons olive oil, Salt & Black Pepper
1 cup frozen Peas
6 tablespoons Heavy Cream, 2 tablespoons butter, Grated Cheese

Place a large frying pan on top of the stove. Add olive oil. Turn heat on to low. Remove the sausage meat from the skin and crumble into small pieces. Cook sausage meat on low heat for 8 minutes.

Add onions sauté for 6 minutes on low heat. Add garlic, cook two minutes.
Drain the oil off of the meat.

Add tomatoes, plus 1 cup of water to pan. Cook on high heat until the tomatoes come to the boil. Lower to a simmer and cook for 45 minutes, stirring sauce occasionally.

Add cream to pan and cook for 10 minutes. Add frozen peas, cook 3 minutes on low heat. The Sauce is done.

Cook the rigatoni, or if you prefer another pasta in rapidly boiling salted water. Cook according to directions on package.

Drain the pasta, reserving a few tablespoons of pasta cooking water. Put pasta and reserved water back in the pot the pasta cooked in. Add butter and mix. Add half the sauce to pot and mix. Serve pasta in equal portions on 4 plates. Top each plate of pasta with remaining sauce. Pass around grated Pecorino or Parmigiano. Enjoy!

ORECCHIETTE SALSICE e RAPINI

Ingredients:

1 lb.Imported Italian Orecchiette
4 links Hot or Sweet Italian Sausge
1 lb. fresh Brocoli Rabe washed and cut into
1 ½" pieces
¼ cup Olive Oil
¼ teaspoon Hot Red Pepper flakes
1/3 cup grated Pecorino
Salt and Black Pepper
4 cloves Garlic peeled and coarsely chopped
1/8 teaspoon Crushed red Pepper Flakes
Fill a large pot with 6-7 qts. Water and bring to boil. Add 3 tablespoons salt to water, then add Broccoli Rabe, cover pot and boil for three minutes.

Remove the broccoli Rabe with a slotted spoon from water and keep on the side.

Place 3 tablespoons olive oil in a large skillet. Add the Sausage and cook over medium heat until the sausage is completely cooked through. As the sausage is cooking, break the sausage with a wooden spoon into pieces that are about a inch-and-a-half around.

Cook Orecchiette in a large part of boiling that are about a inch-and-a-half around.

After the sausage has been cooked through, remove sausage from pan with a slotted spoon and set aside. Add the garlic to pan and a little more olive oil, if needed. Add Pepperoncino. Saute the garlic over medium heat for about two minutes, then add the Broccoli Rabe and sauté for about five minutes over low to medium to heat. Season with Salt & Black Pepper to taste.

Drain cooked Orecchiette from water, reserving 3 tablespoons of water to toss with pasta. Add drained orecchiette and water to pan with Broccoli Rabe. Add sausage, toss and cook over medium heat for two minutes.

Serve 4-6 equal portions on plates or in pasta bowls. Sprinkle olive oil and grated Pecorino over Orecchiette. Serve and enjoy!

PASTA con GALLINA
"Maccheroni with Chicken & Mushrooms"

This Pasta & Chicken dish is quite a rare dish from Sicily. Not many people know of it other than Sicilians and Sicilian-Americans. It's a Secret Recipe you're sure to Enjoy!

6 Chicken Thighs
1 medium Onion, peeled and diced
2 cloves Garlic, peeled and cut in half
16 Button Mushrooms, washed and quartered
6 tablespoons Olive Oil
¼ cup dry White Wine, 1 Egg, Salt & Pepper
¼ cup Pecorino Romano Cheese, grated
¼ cup chopped fresh Italian Parsley
1 pound Rigatoni, or other short pasta

Season Chicken with salt & pepper. Brown the chicken on medium heat with Olive Oil in a medium size pot for 12 minutes. Remove chicken from pan and set aside.

Add mushrooms to pan and cook on medium heat for 5 minutes. Add onions and sauté for 4 minutes on low heat. Add garlic and cook for 2 minutes on low heat.

Put chicken back in pan with the mushrooms & onions. Add wine and cook on medium heat for 4-5 minutes until the wine is reduced by half. Lower heat to low, cover pan, and let cook on low heat for 15 minutes.

Remove from heat and let chicken cool. Once chicken has cooled down, remove meat from chicken thighs. Discard the bones. Put chicken meat back in the pot with mushrooms.

Cook the pasta according to directions on package. Drain pasta, reserving ¼ cup of pasta cooking water. Put reserved water in pot with chicken.

Put the drained pasta in pot with chicken and mix and butter. Mix well.

Beat egg. Add cheese and parsley to egg and mix. Pour this mixture over chicken and pasta. Mix rapidly.

Plate Chicken & Pasta on 4 plates in equal portions for main-course, or 6 plates as a starter or middle course. Enjoy!

LASAGNA

Ingredients For SAUCE:

3-28 oz. cans San Marzano crushed tomatoes
or other good quality Italian style tomatoes
7 cloves minced garlic
1 small onion, minced
½ teaspoon crushed red pepper
¼ cup virgin olive oil
¼ chopped fresh basil or 1 teaspoon dried
Salt and pepper to taste

Remaining Ingredients:

2 lbs. Ronzoni (or other) boxes of Lasagna
2 ½ pound Whole Milk Ricotta
1 ½ pounds Mozzarella
2 ½ cups grated Parmigiano Reggiano
or Grana Padano

In a 6 quart or larger pot, sauté onions over a low
flame for 3 minutes. Add garlic and cook for 3-4
minutes. Do not let the garlic get dark or burn.

Add tomatoes, turn heat up to high and stir. When sauce starts to bubble, turn flame down so the sauce is at a low simmer. Simmer for 45 minutes while frequently stirring the bottom of the pan to keep sauce from burning. Add fresh basil in the last ten minutes of cooking.

As the sauce is cooking. Cook the lasagna sheets. Cook according to directions on lasagna package, but cook 1 minute less the instruction call for. Cook the lasagna in a large pot of rapidly boiling salted water.

Have a large bowl or pot of iced water on the side. As soon as the lasagna sheets are cooked according to instructions, remove from boiling water and place in ice water.

ASSEMBLING THE LASAGNA

Remove lasagna sheets from iced-water and let water drain off in a colander.

Dry the lasagna with a towel. This is very important, you don't want a soggy watery lasagna do you?

Shred or chop the Mozzarella in small pieces.

In a large bowl, mix eggs with the ricotta and ¼ of the grated Parmigiano.

In a 10 x 14 inch pan (or similar), coat the bottom of the pan with tomato sauce. Place sheets of lasagna lengthwise over tomato sauce. Cover the lasagna with more sauce, and sprinkle on a little Parmigiano.

You will now place lasagna sheets that will go from the bottom and up the sides of the lasagna pan and over the to Place sheets on one side of the bottom of the pan and going up and draping over the sides of the pan. Later these sheets will be folded over the top. Do the same on the opposite side of the pan.

Place half of the ricotta cheese mixture as the next layer. Lay sheets of lasagna over the cheese lengthwise in the pan. Press down slightly on pasta. Spread a little tomato sauce over this layer of lasagna sheets, then sprinkle with Parmigiano. Repeat this step again with remaining ricotta to get the second and final layer of ricotta-mozzarella mixture.

Fold over the side lasagna sheets over the top layer on each side. Place the final layer of lasagna sheets over the top of the lasagna lengthwise. Spread tomato sauce over final sheets of pasta. Sprinkle on a generous amount of Parmigano.

Cover Lasagna loosely with aluminum foil and bake at 375 degrees for 45 minutes. Remove aluminum foil and bake a further 25 minutes at 375 degrees.

Remove Lasagna from oven and let rest for 30 minutes before serving.

IMPORTANT NOTES: Make sure that when you are assembling the Lasagna that you have two cups of Tomato Sauce leftover that you will heat up separately from the Lasagna and put some tomato sauce on the bottom of the plate you serve the lasagna on as well as draping a little Tomato Sauce over the top of the plated Lasagna and pass around grated cheese.

It is best to make your lasagna the night before serving. Cook the Lasagna, remove from oven. Let the Lasagna cool down at room temperature for about 90 minutes, then put in refrigerator a cool a few hours or overnight. To reheat the whole pan of lasagna, place in a 400 degree oven for 15 minutes, lower oven to 350 degrees and bake another 25 minutes. Remove from oven and let sit for 15 minutes before cutting and serving with heated Tomato Sauce and grated Parmigiano Reggiano. Enjoy!

SPAGHETTI AGLIO OLIO

GARLIC & OIL ???

Garlic? Oil? Olive Oil that is! And Italian Olive Oil at that, "please." With these two ingredients, Salt and Pepper, ground Black, Pepperoncino or both, you can do quite a lot. Sauté any of the favorite Italian Greens of; Escarole, Green Beans, or Broccoli Rabe (Rapini) and your set. You got a tasty supremely nutritious antipasto or side dish. Italian-Americans love there Escarole and Broccoli Rabe sautéed in garlic and oil just as much as anything, and not far behind the favorites of Sausages and Meatballs, Italian Greens are right up there, and robustly flavored with our prized Italian Olive Oil and Garlic. The following tow dish are the perfect examples of what a little bit of Garlic & Oil can do. You've got the much loved Spaghetti Aglio e Olio

1 pound of imported Italian Spaghetti
¼ cup good quality Italian Olive Oil
6 – 8 cloves Garlic, peeled and thinly sliced
¼ teaspoon Pepperoncino
¼ cup fresh chopped Italian Parsley (Optional)
NO CHEESE !!!

Place Garlic and Olive Oil in a large frying pan. Cook over medium heat for about 4 minutes, just until you see the garlic turn slightly brown. Add red pepper flakes and let cook on the lowest possible flame for minute. Remove from heat.

Cook spaghetti in rapidly boiling water until slightly al dente, which should be about 1 minute under the suggested package time, but you need to test by taking a strand of spaghetti out of the pot and eating it to test the amount of doneness, if it's cooked enough or needs another minute or two. It takes practice and a little know-how, but all good Italians know.

When Spaghetti is done cooking, drain in colander reserving a few tablespoons of pasta cooking water to go in the sauce.

After draining pasta, add to the pan with the Garlic & Oil with the reserved pasta water. Mix spaghetti with garlic and oil. If using Parsley, add now and mix. Serve into 4 equal portions on 4 plates. "Do not pass Cheese" for this dish, it's a No-No!

GOA ? "Spaghetti with Garlic Oil & Anchovies"

GOA, a.k.a. Spaghetti with Garlic Oil & Anchovies, another great-favorite especially with Italian-Americans, "We Love It." To make it, follow the above recipe and simply add 6 – 8 *minced anchovy filets*. Throw the anchovies in about the two minute mark of cooking the garlic and finish as per the rest of the recipe and Voila, you've got a super tasty plate of GOA, Garlic Oil & Anchovies, "Mangia Bene"

CAVATAPPI w/ CAULIFLOWER

1 large head cauliflower, core and cut into
1-1/2" pieces
10 cloves of garlic, peeled
1 - 28 oz. cans crushed San Marzano Tomato's
1 medium onion, minced
½ teaspoon crushed red pepper
¼ cup olive oil, salt and pepper to taste

Place half the oil in a large pot with the minced onions. Sauté for three minutes. Add five cloves of garlic that have been thinly sliced. Sauté for 3 minutes over low heat. Add Red Pepper, sauté for 2 minutes.

Add tomatoes and simmer over low heat for 45 minutes.

While tomato sauce is slowly simmering, place remainder of olive oil in a large frying pan and sauté the cauliflower over medium heat for 12-15 minutes until it is slightly browned.

Add remaining 5 whole garlic cloves with cauliflower. Sauté for about 5 minutes. Add salt & pepper to taste.

Add cauliflower to tomato sauce and cook for 10 minutes.

You can use almost and pasta for this sauce, although short pasta such as rigatoni, Ditalini, orecchietti, or *Cavatappi* work best.

Cook the pasta according to directions on package, drain, pour sauce over pasta and mix.

Serve w/ grated Pecorino Romano, Grana Padano, or Parmigianno Reggiano.

PASTA VRACCULA ARRIMINATU
Pasta with Cauliflower
alla Polizzi Generosa

1 large head cauliflower, core and cut into
1-1/2" pieces
10 cloves of garlic, peeled
1 - 28 oz. cans crushed San Marzano Tomatoes
1 medium onion, minced
½ teaspoon crushed red pepper
¼ cup olive oil, salt and pepper to taste
6 Anchovy Filets, minced fine
1 pinch of Spanish Saffron

Place half the oil in a large pot with the minced onions. Sauté for three minutes. Add five cloves of garlic that have been thinly sliced. Sauté for 3 minutes over low heat. Add Red Pepper, sauté for 2 minutes.

Add tomatoes and simmer over low heat for 30 minutes.

While tomato sauce is simmering, place remainder of olive oil in a large frying pan and sauté the cauliflower over medium heat for 12-15 minutes until it is slightly browned.

Add remaining 5 whole garlic cloves and Anchovy Filets to pan with the cauliflower. Sauté for about 5 minutes. Add salt & pepper to taste.

Add cauliflower to tomato sauce and cook for 10 minutes.

You can use almost and pasta for this sauce, Although short pasta such as rigatoni, Ditalini, Orecchiette, or Cavatappi work best.

Cook the pasta according to directions on package, drain, pour sauce over pasta and mix.

Serve w/ grated, Grana Padano, Pecorino Romano or Parmigianno Reggiano.

MANICOTTI alla Lucia

This is my mothers Manicotti recipe. She made the dish often, and we loved it much. Manicotti, like some of the other dishes in this book, was one of those dishes that way back when, was on practically every single Italian Restaurant menu and the country. It was as they say "deriguer," a required item. As has been the case in past years, you won't see it many an Italian restaurant menu these days other than an old-school Red Sauce Joint, or in people's homes. Italian-Americans still love it, and we eat it now and then. If you want to too, my mom's recipe follows.

3 ½ cups Tomato Sauce
2 tablespoon Butter
1 8-oz. box Manicotti Shells (Ronzoni)
4 cups whole-milk Ricotta
1 cup grated Parmigiano Reggiano
8 tablespoons chopped fresh Italian Parsley
1 1/2 tsp. kosher salt
1/2 tsp. freshly ground black pepper
1 tsp. freshly ground nutmeg
2 eggs, beaten
Grease the bottom and sides of a 10 X 14 baking pan with softened Butter. Add a half cup tomato sauce across the bottom of the pan. Set aside.

Bring a 6-qt. pot of salted water to a boil over high heat. Add the manicotti and cook until just tender, about 8 minutes. Drain manicotti and rinse under cold water; set aside.

Heat oven to 400 degrees. Place all the Ricotta Cheese and half the Parsley in a large glass mixing bowl with salt, pepper, nutmeg, and eggs and stir to combine.

Spoon some of the filling into both openings of each manicotti shell. Repeat with remain-ing manicotti shells.

Transfer stuffed manicotti to prepared baking dish, making 2 rows. Spread the remaining tomato sauce over the manicotti and sprinkle with remaining parmesan. Bake in a 400 degree oven for 15 minutes. Turn heat down to 350 and cook another 15 minutes. Sprinkle with remaining parsley. Let sit for a few minutes before serving. Serve 3 Manicotti per person and enjoy.

Gagootz !!!

It wasn't that long ago when almost every Italian American family would maintain a vegetable garden, reason were two. One being economical, the other being that Italian immigrants own cultural needs of the foods they were used to and wanted. They could get; Olive Oil, dry Pasta, Anchovies, capers, Salami, dried beans lentils and such at their neighborhood Italian Groceria. They could get fresh vegetables, but if the family had any patch of land at all, they'd opt to grow their own. Of course they'd have; tomatoes, eggplant, Italian Parsley, Basil, Peppers, and maybe Green Beans, and Escarole growing in their gardens. If they were lucky, they might keep rabbits, and a few chickens, especially as these fowl could be an endless source of eggs for making themselves Frittata, Sausage & Pepper Sandwiches, and pasta.

I remember back to my very young childhood in the mid 60's when we'd go to my mother's friend house, the Santangelo's in Garfield, New Jersey, and they had one such vegetable garden where they had these weird looking trees, that had been pruned low with their big branches cut right off (Fig Trees). They also had a big pergola with grapes hanging down, and their garden was filled with all the prerequisite vegetable for an Italian-American family. Yes, they had; Tomatoes, peppers, Melanzane (Eggplant), Scarola, Zucchini, and those big as a Baseball Bat squash called "Gagootz" (Cucuzza) of which they'd make; soup, pasta sauces, or Stufato di Gagootz (Cucuazza Stew). To a large extent, the prevalence of these Italian Family Vegetable Gardens have waned, yet thank God not disappeared completely. Some still do it, and it's gaining in popularity, as is the great Italian-American tradition and ritual of making your own wine. Even if you didn't have a backyard, and lived in an apartment down in the Village, you might have a few buckets, and at least grow your own Basil and Tomatoes, perhaps a bucket of Peppers as well. It's a fine old tradition.

But those Gagootz, they fascinated me so when I was a kid and I'd be in back of the Santgelo's backyard garden, among the Sun Flowers, Grapevines, and Gagootz, it was magical, and an Italian-American thing to be sure. But hey, if you got some land, you can grow some, and continue these great traditions of our grandparents before us, like my mothers parents Josephina and Philipo Bellino, who came from Sicily with Cuccuzza seeds from Sicily, that he would plant in America.

Hey, I almost forgot. Speaking of Cacuzza, I even knew a girl named Caccuzza (Spelled a little different). Wow! No, it wasn't her nickname, though it might be for some, if you know what I mean? No that was her families surname, Caccuzza, and her name was Rose Caccuzza.

Pasta e Cuccuzza

Here's a recipe from my good buddy Chris Cordaro who has what is billed as the Largest Italian Cuccuzza Grower Plantation in the World. Chris is a Sicilian American from Louisiana. His Cuccuzza are prized by Chefs and Italian Ameri-cans all over the country. I know they are shipped to the Hunts Point Market in the Bronx, New York, to long Island, and the Paterson Market in New Jersey for all us Sicilians, Neapolitans, and Calabrese folks who don't grow our own, but never-the-less we need Chris's Cuccuzza's for our Pasta Gagootz, Cuccuzza Caponata, and Cuccuzza Stew and Soup. Other Italians eat Cuccuzza too, but none as much those of us of Sicilian ancestry like Chris, his family, and all the many Sicilians in New Orleans and other parts of the great state of Louisiana, of which more Sicilians immigrated to than any other part of America, even New York or Philadelphia. You may well know of the Lupo family (also Sicilian) of New Orleans who created the famed Muffuletta Sandwich at the

Central Grocery in the French Quarter of New Orleans. So, anyway, Chris is Sicilian in a state has a lot of Sicilians. His grandfather brought the seeds from Sicily that the Cordero's grow their famed Cucuzza's with today, the rest is history as they say.

PASTA con CUCUZZA e FAVE

Ingredients:

¼ cup Olive Oil
1 Onion, peeled and dice
4 cloves Garlic, peeled and chopped
1 medium Cucuzza, peeled & cut in 1 & ½ " dice
½ cup water
1 cup Frozen or Fresh Fava Beans (or Lima Beans)
½ teaspoon Salt & ½ teaspoon Black Pepper
2 cups Tomato Sauce
¼ cup fresh Basil
1 pound Ditalini, or other short pasta you like
½ cup grated Pecorino Romano Cheese

Place onion in a large pot with olive oil, cook over low heat for 10 minutes. Add garlic & Fava Beans and cook 2 minutes.

Add Cucuzza and cook 4 minutes. Add tomatoes and water. Cook on low heat for 25 minutes. Add basil after the cucuzza has been cooking for 20 minutes.

While the Cucuzza is cooking, cook the pasta according to directions on package.

Drain the pasta, reserving ½ cup of pasta water that you will add to the cucuzza. Add pasta to cucuzza and let cook for 5 minutes.

Serve, and pass around the grated Pecorino Cheese, and drizzle a bit of Olive Oil on top.

And, as Chris or almost any good Italian would do, serve with some nice crusty Italian Bread on the side.

The Cordaro Cucuzza Plantation, Ruston, LA
The World's Largest Gowers of Italian Cucuzza Squash .... http://www.cucuzzasquash.com

You can buy Fresh Louisiana Cucuzza from the Cordaro family, along with Basil & Cucuzza Seeds, and tasty Cucuzza Blossom Honey.

CUCUZZA FRIES: Peel Cucuzza and cut into French Fry shapes. Dip into a mixture of beaten eggs, then into flour that's seasoned with Salt & Pepper. Shake off excess and fry in hot oil. Drain put in a glass bowl, season with salt and serve.

Recipes for Pasta con Cucuzza and *French Fried Cucuzza,* courtesy of Chris Cordaro.

Note: "Gagootz" is Neapolitan and Italian-American slang for Cucuzza.

BUCATINI all AMATRICIANA

INGREDIENTS:

3 medium onions, sliced thinly
¼ cup olive oil, 3 cloves garlic, minced
1 teaspoon crushed Red Pepper flakes
1 lb. smoked bacon and ½ lb. pancetta diced
2-28 oz. cans crushed tomatoes
Sea Salt and Black Pepper to taste
1 & 1/2 lbs. Bucatini or other pasta

Place bacon and pancetta in a large frying pan and cook over very low heat to render fat (about 12 minutes). Do not brown or let bacon get hard or crispy.

Remove bacon and pancetta from pan and set aside. Drain all but 3 tablespoons of fat from pan. Add olive oil and onions to pan and sauté over low heat for about 12 minutes. Add garlic and red pepper, sauté for three minutes. Add tomato's, bacon, and pancetta. Simmer for 40 minutes.

Cook Bucatini or other pasta. Drain pasta, sprinkle with olive oil. Add sauce, mix and plate. Serve with grated Parmigiano.

"Danny Bolognese's" BOLOGNESE

This is the recipe for my justly famous Bolognese Sauce, or as it is known in Italy, Ragu Bolognese. The Journal of Italian Food & Wine magazine once did an article on me and my restaurant Bar Cichetti, where they wrote that my Bolognese was the best in the country. Many agree. My nickname is actually, Danny Bolognese. That might tell you something about my Bolognese, and that's it's so unbelievably tasty, it's practically *orgasmic.* "We kid you not."

The great Italian Cookbook Author, Marcella Hazan once stated, "The marriage of fresh-made Tagiatelle Pasta and a perfectly made Ragu Bolognese is one of the most ethereal taste in the entire culinary World." We'd definitely agree Marcella, and mine, and when I make it, it surely fits the bill.

This dish is not hard to make, though you think it might be. Well, if you do not have a great recipe, and do not know how to make it, yes it might be. But here you go, one of the World's greatest recipes for the sauce of which it has been said, "is among the best in the world," America anyway.

Make it, and with this recipe and a bit of practice, you'll get it, and you can be famous in your circle of friends and family, in having *The Best Bolognese.*

Bravo!

The Recipe:

2 tablespoons olive oil
1 medium onion, minced
 2 celery stalks & I carrot minced
2 lbs. ground beef and 1 lb. ground veal
3 cups red wine, 1 cup chicken broth
2-28 ounce cans crushed San Marzano Tomatoes
1 oz. dried Porcini Mushrooms, soak in hot water for10 minutes to soften Mushrooms
5 tablespoons of sweet butter
2 sprigs fresh Rosemary and 2 of Sage, tied together

Put olive oil, celery, onion, and minced carrot in a large pot. Sauté over a low flame for 5 minutes. Add ground meats to pot and cook until the meat has lost its raw color. Do not brown the meat or it will get hard. Break the meat up with a wooden spoon as you are cooking it.

Drain the fat off the meat mixture in a strainer. Put the drained meat back in the pot and season with Salt and Pepper.

Add wine and cook over high heat until the wine is reduced by half. Add tomatoes, Porcini and broth.

Cook the sauce over the lowest flame possible for 2 ½ hours while stirring every few minutes to keep the sauce from burning. Add the fresh Rosemary & Sage in the last 30 minutes of cooking.

When sauce is finished cooking, turn off flame and stir butter into sauce. Remove the rosemary & sage and discard.

Cook the pasta of your choice, Tagiatelle is most traditional for Bolognese Sauce, but you may use Spaghetti, Rigatoni, or Fusilli.

Drain the cooked past and mix it with some of the sauce and a knob of butter. Serve with grated Parmigiano Reggiano Cheese.

CLEMENZA'S
MOB WAR SUNDAY SAUCE

"Hey come over here kid. Learn something. You never know when you're gonna have to cook for 20 guys some day. You see, you start out with a little oil. Then you fry some garlic. Then you throw in some tomatoes, tomato paste, you fry it, you make sure it doesn't stick. You get it to a boil. You Shove in your Sausage and Meatballs, Hey? Add a bit of Wine, a little sugar, you see? And that's my trick."

Peter Clemenza, The Godfather

Sunday Sauce, a.k.a. Gravy is the most supreme dish of all of Italian-American. It's made every Sunday in hundreds of Italian Households in Italian strongholds like; Brooklyn, The North End of Boston, Phladelphia, New Orleans, Chicago, and all over New Jersey, and wherever Italians may be in America. The Gravy (Sunday Sauce), we hold in high-reverence. And why not, it's got Meatballs, Sausages, Braciole and all our favorite things to eat, all-in-one. Sunday Sauce is oh so tasty, and it's a dish that brings the whole family together each and every Sunday.

There are a number of ways to make Sunday Sauce (Gravy) and ingredients may vary, though the basic premise is the same, of; two or more meats slowly braised in tomato sauce. Here, in Clemenza's Recipe, he makes the most basic Gravy there is, with just Sausages & Meatballs, but believe me, that's enough, and with the more meats, it's just like *Guilding The Lilly.* Actually, the one most popular way to make Gravy, is with Braciola (Braciole), whereby you would make this recipe of Clemenza's and just add Braciola to it.

Sunday Sauce, is legendary and mythical, but it's not that hard to make. If you've never made one before, now is high time. Just start hear with Clemenza's Secret Recipe Mob War Sunday Sauce from the Godfather, just like Michael and his dad's Caporegime, Pete Clemnza. You can even make it for 20 guys some day. "Mangia Bene

LUCIA'S JERSEY BRACIOLA

When I was a young boy, I'd watch my mother making Meatballs and Braciole for the Gravy. She'd have some flank steak laid out on the counter, season them with salt and pepper, and lay on garlic, raisons, Pignoli Nuts, breadcrumbs, and Pecorino Cheese before rolling them-up and tying them with string so they wouldn't fall apart as they slowly cooked in the Sauce. She'd then brown them, before putting them in the sauce to cook. Then I'd watch her make the meatballs. I'd help her to roll them up. She'd fry the meatballs a bit before putting them in the Sauce that was already simmering with the Braciole for a couple hours. After the meatballs were browned, they'd go in the Gravy to finish cooking for a half-hour. Then the Sauce was ready, and we'd be ready to eat. "Yumm!!!"

INGREDIENTS:

1 - 1/2 pounds Beef Flank Steak (cut the beef on an angle in pieces approximately 3 ½" by 6 ½")
6 cloves garlic, peeled and chopped
½ cup Parsley, washed dried & chopped
¼ Cup Grated Pecorino Romano Cheese
¼ cup Bread Crumbs, plain
Olive Oil, 2 Tbs. Pignoli Nuts
Raisons, Sea Salt & Black Pepper
Once the beef has been cut, lay all the pieces out on a clean table. Lightly season the beef with salt & pepper.

Drizzle a little olive oil over each piece of beef. Evenly distribute chopped Parsley over all the Beef.

Evenly distribute the Pecorino Cheese over all the beef.

Sprinkle Bread Crumbs over Beef. Put raisons and Pignoli Nuts on to each slice of Beef.

Roll each piece of beef Jelly-Roll style. Take two toothpicks for each piece of beef and fasten each piece of beef closed with the toothpicks.

Lightly salt & pepper the outside of each rolled piece of beef.

Brown all the Beef Rolls (Braciole) in a pan with Olive Oil. Once all the beef is nicely browned, put all the Beef Braciole into tomato sauce or meat gravy that you have already started.

MEATBALLS alla CLEMENZA

RECIPE:

1 lb. ground Beef
½ lb. ground Veal, ½ lb. Ground Pork
4 Tbs. fresh Italian Parsley, chopped
1 minced onion, 2 cloves garlic, minced
4 Tablespoons plain breadcrumbs
2 large eggs, ¼ cup Milk
Salt & Pepper, ½ cup grated Parmigiano

In a small bowl, break and beat eggs. Add breadcrumbs and milk and let soak for 10 minutes.

In a large bowl, add all the remaining ingredients. Add eggs and mix well with your hands.

Shape meat mixture to from balls that are about 3 inches in diameter.

Coat the bottom of a cookie sheet or roasting pan with a thin film of olive oil. Cook Meatballs at 350 degrees for 10 minutes.

Take meatballs out of oven and simmer on low heat for 45 minutes in a batch of Tomato Sauce or Sunday Sauce (Gravy).

Mob War Sauce alla Clemenza

How to Make It. The SAUCE !!!

INGREDIENTS:

10 to 12 Sweet or Hot Italian Pork Sausages
1 medium Onion, peeled and chopped fine
8 Cloves garlic, peeled and finely chopped
¼ Cup Olive Oil
5-28 ounce Cans Whole San Marzano Tomatoes or other good quality tomatoes. Puree or finely chop 3 of the cans of tomatoes and leave 2 cans tomatoes chunky 1/2 small can Tomato Paste
1 teaspoon Pepperoncino
1 tablespoon each of Slat & Black Pepper
1 teaspoon Sugar
And a Bit O' Wine (1/4 cup Red Wine)
1 Batch of *Meatballs* from the preceding recipe

Brown the Sausages in a large pot with 3 tablespoons olive oil, over medium heat for about 8-10 minutes. Remove to a plate and set aside.

Add remaining olive oil to pot. Lower heat to low. Add the garlic and cook for about 3 minutes.

"Add Tomato Paste Fry with Garlic. You make sure it doesn't stick" (just like Clemenza). *"Add your tomatoes, continue frying, Then you Shove-In your Sausage & Meatballs, add o' bit of Wine, a little Sugar, and that's Clemenza's Trick."*

Simmer for 1 ½ hour at lowest heat level possible and it's done, *Sunday Sauce alla Clemenza.*

GRAVY

Gravy, Sunday Sauce, "what's the difference?" There is none, it's just two different names for the same things. Some even simply call it *Sauce,* like Clemenza did in the Godfather. Some say Sunday Gravy, some say Sunday Sauce, some say, "Gravy," while some just call it Sauce. In the New York and New Jersey area where we grew up, we called it Gravy. No matter what you call it, it's one of the World's tastiest dishes ever.

BROOKLYN STYLE GRAVY
Fuhgettabout-It !!!

To make the most popular *Gravy* of all, all you have to do is combine the three previous recipes of Clemenza's Meatballs & Sausage Sunday Suace Gravy with Braciola.

You will start Clemenza's Sauce, but you might want to add one extra can of tomatoes for a total of 6 – 28 cans of San Marzano or other similar tomatoes. If you do you will want to increase the amount of Garlic to 10 cloves, or even 12 if you like more.

Once you get the tomato sauce going, you'll start on the Braciole. Follow the Braciola recipe, make the filling and roll-up the Braciole, securing them with toothpicks or tyin10g with string. Brown the Braciole to a nice golden brown, then add them to the slow simmering sauce and let them cook for an hour and a half, before adding the meatballs.

Take a little break. Drink a little Wine. After the Braciole has been in the pot for a half hour, brown the Sausages lightly in a pan for about 8 minutes. Place the sausages in the Gravy, and it's on to the Meatballs.

Make the meatballs from Clemenza's recipe. Brown them lightly, then add to the Gravy that has been cooking for at least two hours by now. After you brown the meatballs, add to the Gravy and cook just about twenty minutes, and your sauce is done.

VERDURE

Verdure, as they're known in Italy, vegetables over here. We love them. Many non-Italians might not know that along with pasta, vegetables are a cornerstone of the Italian Diet and Italian Cuisine of which is based on vegetables more than any other cuisine in the world. True! We eat a lot of them, and you should too. Get your 6 servings of fruits and vegetables every day. That's the U.S. Surgeon Generals rule. We always get ours, with; Salad and the greens we Italians love so; Broccoli Rabe and Escarole, aka *Scarola.* We've included a few good ones here, like; Eggplant Parmigiano, Giambotto, Funghetto, and my famous *Secret Recipe* Eggplant Caponata, or as my Aunts called it, Caponatina. These are some great recipes! Go for it!

GIAMBOTTO alla NAPOLITANA

Ingredients:

8 tablespoons Olive Oil
2 Green Bell Peppers, core & seeds removed
2 medium Onions, peeled and chopped
6 cloves Garlic, peeled and sliced
½ teaspoon Sea Salt, 1 teaspoon Black Pepper
1 /2 teaspoon Red Pepper Flakes
1 28 ounce can Plum Tomatoes
1 medium Eggplant, washed and cut to 1 ½ "
cubes
2 Zucchini, cut into 2 inch cubes
2 Idaho Potatoes, peeled and cubed

Cut Green Peppers into 2 " squares. Place peppers in a medium size pot with olive oil. Cook at low heat for 10 minutes. Add onions and cook at low heat for 4 minutes. Add garlic salt, Black Pepper, and red pepper flakes and cook at low heat for 3 minutes. Add tomatoes and cook at medium heat for 6 minutes.

Cook potatoes in boiling salted water for 4 minutes at a rapid boil. Drain and set aside.

Add eggplant to pot with tomatoes and cook for 8 minutes. Add potatoes and cook at low heat for 3 minutes.

Add Zucchinini and cook 12 minutes. Your Giambotto is ready to serve.

FUNGHETTO

Funghetto is an Italian way of cooking mushrooms with garlic, oil, and parsley. You can cook cook Eggplant or Zucchini in the same manner. Whereby the eggplant would be called Melanzane al Funghetto and the zucchini will be Zucchini al Funghetto.

4 cups medium Button Mushrooms
8 tablespoons Olive Oil
5 Garlic Cloves, peeled and sliced
¼ cup chopped fresh Italian Parsley
¼ teaspoon each of Salt & Black Pepper

Cut Mushrooms into 4 pieces each so they look like wedges. Cook mushrooms in a large frying pan with Olive Oil on high flame for 7 minutes. Do in two batches if your pan is not large enough.

Add garlic and Red Pepper and cook at high heat 2 minutes. Turn heat to medium cook for 3 minutes.

Add Salt & Pepper cook 1 minute while mixing with a wooden spoon. Turn heat off. Add Parsley and mix. Serve as an Antipasto item or side dish to poultry, meat, or fish.

CAPONATA SICILIANA

INGREDIENTS:

2 large eggplants, washed and cut into
¾" cubes, do not remove skin from Eggplant
½ cup olive oil
3 medium onions, cut into ¼" dice
1 small Red Pepper and 1 Yellow Pepper
Cut into ½" dice, 2 Celery stalks, ¼" dice
¼ raisons, soak in hot water for 15 minutes
1 ½ cups Tomato Sauce
6 tablespoons sugar
6 tablespoons Balsamic vinegar
2 teaspoons Kosher or Sea Salt
3 teaspoons Black Pepper
3 tablespoons of Capers

Sauté the peppers in a large pot with ½ of the olive oil for 10 minutes

Add the onions and sauté over low heat for 15 minutes.

Add the celery and tomato sauce and continue simmering. While the other ingredients are simmering, brown the Eggplant in several batches in a large frying pan with remaining olive oil. Add the browned Eggplant, sugar, and vinegar to the pot and simmer for 25 minutes over very low heat. Cool and serve on its own, as a topping for Crostini, as part of an Antipasto Misto, or as an accompaniment to any Grilled or Roast Fish, with Lamb, or with Grilled Chicken.

EGGPLANT PARMIGIANO

Eggplant Parmigiano was big in our family. We're Sicilian, and along with Neapolitans Sicilians eat more eggplant than any other Italians. My Aunt Fran's was the tastiest in our whole family of pretty good cooks. I loved it, and when I started cooking the dish myself, it was aunt Fran's recipe I got. Here it is below.

RECIPE:

7 cups Tomato Sauce (from recipe in book)
Salt and freshly ground black pepper
1 ½ cups Flour, 3 eggs
1 1/2 cups plain Bread Crumbs
1 large Eggplant
12 fresh Basil leaves, torn into pieces
1 ¼ cups grated Parmigiano Reggiano

Place flour in a shallow dish. Beat eggs together in another shallow dish. Mix breadcrumbs with a pinch of salt & pepper in a third shallow dish. Set dishes aside.

Peel and trim eggplant and slice lengthwise into 1/2" pieces. Dredge each slice first in the flour, then in the egg, then in the seasoned bread crumbs.

Put oil in a large frying pan, and heat to medium-high heat until oil is hot but not smoking. Add breaded eggplant slices to the hot oil (work in batches, if needed) and cook until golden on both sides and dark brown on the edges, 2 -3 minutes per-side.

Spread a thin layer of tomato sauce in the bottom of a large shallow ovenproof dish. Arrange eggplant in a single layer on top of tomato sauce. Spoon remaining sauce over eggplant. Sprinkle with Parmigiano Reggiano, then provolone. Bake in a 400 degree oven for 15 minutes. Turn heat down to 350 and bake another 20 minutes.

Remove Eggplant from oven and let stand for 8 minutes before serving. Most people eat Eggplant Parmigiano as a main-course, but it's also great as an Antipasto item, whereby you will serve a portion 1/3 to half the size of a main-course. Bon Appetito!

Caponata Napoletana
alla Giovanni

On my second trip to the motherland, I was spending a couple days in la Bella Napoli (Naples) before moving on to the Isle of Capri and on to Positano, two of the most spots on Gods good Earth. I was walking around the city one day, and had made my way of to the Castel Ovo (Egg Castel) at the harbor, which is in the Bay of Naples. You could see Mount Vesuvio in the distance from here. There is a walk way and road that lead out onto the small island that this fortress castle lies on. Besides the Castel Ovo, there is a marina here, along with a few lovely seafood restaurants. I was walking around and was behind one of the restaurants, when I spotted an old man sitting at a small table. He saw me and started talking to me and asked me where I was from. His name was Giovanni. We were chatting a bit, I asked Giovanni where he learned to speak English so well, and he told me he lived in Johannesburg for 20 years and was a cook at a diamond mine there in South Africa. Giovanni was in the back cleaning mussels of which this restaurant specialized in and had numerous dishes made with Cozze (Mussels), like; Cozze Riepieno, Cozze al Posillipo, Spaghetti con Cozze, and Caponata al Napolteana, a dish I'd never seen before, and never ever saw on any menu or in anyone's home in America. Giovanni, said, "why don't you eat here?" I told I already had lunch, but would come for dinner that evening. Which I did. Giovanni wasn't there, he's an old man, goes in in the morning, and finished up by three and goes home. He wasn't there, but he told the waiter about me, that I might stop by, so when I came in he was expecting me. I sat down at a table outside right next to the water, the Bay of Naples. I got a glass nice Greco di Tufo local wine to start and talked to the waiter about what I might have for dinner. He recommended the Caponata and Spaghetti con Cozze which he said were specialties of the house and the two most popular dishes on the menu. How could I not go with his suggestions?

I sipped my Greco di Tufo and took in the wondrous scene before me. I was in Italy, in the animated (misunderstood) city of Napoli, at a restaurant that specialized in Mussels (you don't find many if any of these) sitting outside behind the breathtaking Bay of Naples with Ischia and Capri out in the not too far distance, sipping my glass of local white wine and about to eat a marvelously unique dinner. Life doesn't get much better than this.

A few minutes went by and the waiter brought out my Caponata. Unlike Sicilian Eggplant Caponata, this was much different. I looked at it, and it looked marvelous. This Caponata is a salad of ripe San Marzano Tomatoes, celery, big fat Cerignola Olives, Capers, Mussels, and Frisella.

I dug in. It was amazing! I love it. I'd never seen this dish before, and at the time I was heavily into major explorations of truly authentic Italian Food and cuisine. At the time, I was working (cooking) at my first Italian restaurant in New York, Caio Bella. Well I really enjoyed the Caponata, and then the waiter brought me my Spaghetti con Cozze, spaghetti with mussels in a light marinara sauce. With the local mussels (Cozze) from the nearby Mediterranean Sea, this pasta dish was perfect.

Well that dinner was amazing, and one of the most memorable of my entire life and eating in every corner of the world. I'll never forget that dinner, and still remember it with fondness some 28 years later, absolutely wonderful.

Caponata alla Giovanni

Ingredients for 4:

10 Frisella, or Croutons, see note below
20 large Cerignola or other large
un-pitted Green Olives
2 stalks of Celery, washed and cut
in large chunks
1 large Potato, boiled until soft, then sliced
1 ½ pounds PIE Mussels, washed
¼ cup Sicilian Capers
4 large perfectly rip Salad Tomatoes,
cut in wedges
6 tablespoons Olive Oil
1 ½ tablespoon Red Wine Vinegar
Sea Salt & Black Pepper to taste

Place Mussels in a large pot with 1 cup water.
Turn heat on to high. Cover pot with a top.
Water will boil and steam the mussels. You must
mix the mussels around from time to time with a
wooden spoon, but keep cover when not mixing.
Mussels are done when all the shells open. This
should just take 5-6 minutes. Reserve 8
tablespoons of mussel cooking broth for salad.
Discard any mussels that have not opened. Set
aside and let cool.

When cool set aside 1/3 of the mussels. Remove the mussels from the shell of the remaining 2/3 's of the mussels. Discard the shells.

Soak frisella in water for 1 minute and remove. Place one each whole frisella (Crouton) on bottom of 4 plates. Drizzles with a little olive oil and a bit of vinegar.

Put celery, capers, tomatoes, Olives, Olive Oil, 1 tablespoon of Vinegar, Mussels and reserved mussels cooking water in a large bowl and mix. Take 6 remaining frisella and break into pieces and add to bowl. Mix everything well.

Evenly divide the contents of the bowl over the four plates with 1 whole piece of frisella. Take the remaining third of the Mussels that are still in their shells and dived equally on to the 4 plates.

Serve and enjoy. This is a special dish that most likely your guest have *never seen*. They're gonna love it.

Note: *Frisella*, a.k.a. *Ships Biscuit* is a hardened dry bread from Naples. Sailors would bring on their boats and when ready to eat, they'd dip the bread into sea water to soften. If you can't get your hands on any, make croutons with whole slices of Italian bread that you rub with a raw piece of garlic.

SHRIMP SCAMPI

Shrimp Scampi is one of the All-Time greatest and beloved dishes of the Italian-American repertoire. This dish was insanely popular in Italian-American Restaurants in the 1960's and 70's. There are many old-timers around who love it to this very day, as you and anyone you make it for will as well. It's super tasty, so enjoy.

INGREDIENTS:

2 lbs. large Shrimp, peeled and deveined
5 tablespoons Olive Oil
4 tablespoons Butter
4 cloves Garlic, peeled and sliced thin
Sea Salt and Black Pepper
¼ cup dry White Wine
Juice from 1 Lemon
¼ Chopped Italian Parsley

Heat a large frying pan on medium heat. Add Olive Oil and half the butter. Add Garlic and cook until garlic just starts to show a slight brown color. Turn the heat to high and add Shrimp. Cook until all the shrimp lose their raw color.

Remove the Shrimp to warm plate and keep on the side. Add wine and turn heat up high. Cook until wine is reduced by half.

Add lemon juice and cook 30 seconds. Add remaining butter. Turn heat to high and cook for 30 seconds. Add shrimp and cook over high heat for 1 minute.

Turn off heat, add Parsley and stir. Serve Shrimp Scampi on its own, with steamed spinach, Rice Pilaf, or whatever you like. Enjoy!

JERSEY BAKED BLUEFISH
"alla LUCIA"

Bluefish was plentiful when we were kids. In fact, it still is. We always had neighbors who'd go fishing on party boats down the Jersey Shore. When the Bluefish were running (or mackerel) whoever went fish, caught a ton of fish. Well, maybe not a ton, but quite a lot and too much to eat for themselves, so they'd always give away some nice fresh fish to their neighbors. When didn't eat Bluefish all year, except in the Summertime when the neighbors across the street caught a bunch and gave one to my mom. Her recipe follows.

RECIPE:

4 fresh Bluefish Filets, about 8 ounces each
8 tablespoons Olive Oil
Salt & Black Pepper
6 cloves Garlic, peeled and sliced thin
2 Baking Potatoes, peeled and thickly sliced
1 ½ teaspoons Dry Oregano
1 small Onion, peeled and minced fine

2 Jersey Beefsteak Tomatoes (if in Season)Par-Boil Potatoes in boiling water for exactly 2 minutes. Drain and let cool.

Cover the bottom of a small Pyrex or Ceramic Baking Pan with 1/3 the Olive Oil. Cover bottom of pan with the potato slices. Season the potatoes with salt & pepper. Sprinkle a third of the olive oil over the potatoes.

Sprinkle the minced onions over the potatoes. Place the Bluefish filets over the potatoes. Season the fish with salt & pepper and sprinkle equal portions of the Oregano over each piece of fish.

Preheat oven to 375 degrees. Place half the sliced garlic over the 4 pieces of fish.

Thinly slice tomatoes and cover the fish with equal portions of tomato. Season tomatoes with a little salt & pepper. Sprinkle remaining; Oregano, Olive Oil, and garlic over the tomatoes.

Bake fish at 375 degrees until fish is cooked through. About 20 minutes.

Serve as is or with sautéed escarole, Broccoli Rabe, or a Green Salad on the side. Mangia Bene!

CACCIUCO CARNEVALE
Tuscan Coast Fish Stew

Now here's a tasty dish that just about anyone would love. Any who loves seafood that is! Can you believe that there are actually people who don't like fish or seafood of any kind? Can't be Southern Italian. Anyway, Cacciuco is the famed fish stew of the Coastal areas of Tuscan, with the port city of Livorno in particular. We put in a great recipe from our friend Vincenzo who lives in the seaside resort town of Viareggio, home to many wonderful seafood restaurants, as well as one of the World's premier spots for Carnival, 4th only to those in Rio de Janiero, Venice, and New Orleans.

Vincenzo's recipe is oh so tasty, and not that hard to make. It's a great dish for dinner parties, or any time at all. Mangia Bene!

RECIPE CACCIUCO CARNEVALE

INGREDIENTS:

8 Tablespoons Olive Oil, preferably Tuscan
1 medium Onion, peeled and minced
2 stalks Celery, cut into 1 /2 " pieces
1 Idaho Potato, peeled and sliced
7 cloves Garlic, peeled and sliced thin
1/ teaspoon Red Pepper Flakes
1 – 28 oz. can San Marzano Plum Tomatoes
 2 tablespoons tomato paste
6 cups water, 1 Bay Leaf
½ cup Dry White Wine
1 pound PIE Mussels
18 Littleneck Clams
1 pound medium Shrimp, peeled and deveined
12 large Sea Scallops
1 - ½ pounds filet fresh white fleshed fish; Grouper, Monkfish, or Scrod .. Cut into 8 equal pieces
¼ cup Italian Parsley, wash & roughly chopped
Sea Salt & Black Pepper

Place Olive Oil, Onion, and Celery in a large no-corrosive pot. Cook on low heat for 8 minutes, stirring occasionally. Add garlic and cook 2 minutes. Add Red Pepper and cook two minutes.

Drain the whole pieces of tomato, and reserve the tomato water from can on the side. Turn heat to high and put the drained tomatoes in the pot. Cook on high heat for 4-5 minutes while breaking the whole tomatoes into smaller chunks with a wooden spoon.

Add water and bay Leaf and continue cooking on high heat until the liquid comes to a boil. Add potatoes and let cook on medium simmer for 14 minutes. Lower heat to low simmer.

While this is simmering, put clams and ¼ cup of water in another pot. Cook on high heat until all the clams open, about 7 minutes. If any clams don't open, discard. Take off heat and pot in a bowl to cool. Pour broth from clams in pot with tomatoes.

Place Mussels in the same pot you cooked the clams in. Add the wine and a half cup of water and 1 bay leaf. Cover pot and cook on high heat until all the mussels open. Throw out any mussels that don't open. Leave mussels in pot and let cool.

Add the pieces of fish filet to the pot with tomatoes and cook on low heat for 4 minutes. Add the Scallops and cook for 2 minutes.

Add the shrimp and cook three minutes on very low heat. Turn heat off.

Take half of the mussels out of the pot and remove the mussels from their shells and put in pot with tomatoes and other fish. Throw out mussel shells. Pour the mussel broth in pot with tomatoes and fish.

Add half the Parsley, the clams in their shells and the mussels in their shells to pot and simmer over very low heat for 4 minutes.

Place one large crouton into 4 – 6 bowls. Drizzle a little olive oil over crouton. Put some Cacciuco into each bowl, making sure that each person gets a piece of fish filet, some mussels, clams, shrimp, and scallops. Drizzle a little more olive oil over stew and sprinkle a little Parsley over the top of each bowl of Cacciuco. Enjoy!

LEMON CHICKEN "RAO'S STYLE"

Rao's is the infamous East Harlem Italian Eatery that is filled with Celebrities, Wise Guys and Wannabes. And guess what? You probably can't get in. Know why? Cause "Frankie No" says "No!" It's reserved for VIP, Celebs and those connected to Frankie, one Frank Pelligrino from Goodfellas and Soprano fame. You see, Frankie owns the place. Try if you will, it's the *hardest table in town* and it's all the way up in East Harlem, not downtown or Mid-Town Manhattan. If you ever get in, cherish the experience, if not, here's a recipe for their Famous Lemon Chicken. Make the Chicken, put on some Sinatra, Dino, Jerry Vale, and pretend. Pretend you're at Rao's of New York, a place you probably "*can't get in.*"

The RECIPE!

1 cup fresh lemon juice
1 cup extra-virgin olive oil
1 tbsp. red wine vinegar
1 clove garlic, peeled and minced
1/2 tsp. dried oregano

Salt and freshly ground black pepper
1/4 cup chopped fresh parsley
1 Broiler Chicken, cut into 10 pieces; 2 wings,
2 legs, 2 thighs, and cut the 2 breast in half making
4 pieces

Season the chicken pieces with salt and black pepper.

Place all ingredients except the chicken, a quarter of the olive oil, and the parsley in a large glass or ceramic bowl. Set aside

Turn oven on to 450 degrees.

Put a large frying pan that will be large enough to hole all the chicken on stove top. Turn heat on high. Add ¼ of the olive oil to frying pan. Heat 2 minutes, then add the chicken.

Brown chicken in frying pan for 12, turning the chicken pieces every 4 minutes or so until nicely browned. Place chicken in oven and cook for 15 minutes.

Add the lemon mixture to pan with chicken. Return to over and cook for 12 minutes.

Remove chicken from oven and peek into the inside of the chicken with a knife to make sure the chicken is cooked through and there is no blood. If there is blood, put chicken back in oven and let cook more until there is no more sign of blood on inside of chicken.

Place chicken on a place and keep warm in the oven turned down to 250 degree. Set frying pan with lemon juice mixture from chicken on top of the stove and cook over high heat for minutes. Remove from flame. Let cool down to warm for 5 minutes, then pour a little of the sauce over chicken and set the rest of the lemon sauce on the side. Sprinkle the fresh chopped Parsley over the chicken, serve and enjoy.

POLLO MARENGO
alla Bonaparte

They say the dish is French. Some say it's Italian. Well, the dish was created by a French Chef in Italy. In Marengo, Italy in Piedmont in fact. And for none other than Napoleon Bonaparte after he defeated the Austrian Army at The Battle of Marengo. Legend has it, that Napoleon wasn't in the habit of eating before battle. After Napoleon's Army defeated the Austrians at Marengo in 1800, Napoleon was famished. He was starving, and he commanded his Chef to whip something up. Chef Dumand frantically foraged for ingredients to cook Napoleon's meal. He came up with; chicken, eggs, garlic, crayfish, and a handful of tomatoes. He already had some wine. Dumand made the dish, and gave it to Napoleon. He loved it and commanded it served to him after every battle. The rest is history, so to speak.

Chicken Marengo is an wonderful dish that was pretty popular once-upon-a-time. Not anymore, but we don't know why, it's absolutely awesome! The original dish was made with crayfish which some people still use, but most use Shrimp instead, as we do here in our recipes.

The dish does not call for mushrooms, but they are a nice addition if you like.

Be aware that Chef Dumand after awhile tried to do this, and Napoleon went nuts. He would not have the dish change, as he felt it was bad like. Try this dish, we're sure you'll love it as General and later Emperor Napoleon did. "It's a Winner!"

RECIPE:

1 2 ½ pound Chicken, cut into 8 pieces
½ cup Flour
4 tablespoons Olive Oil
1 tablespoon Butter
1 medium Onion, peeled and chopped
2 cloves Garlic, peeled and sliced
¼ cup Sherry or Dry White Wine
½ teaspoon each of Salt & Black Pepper
4 whole Plum Tomatoes from a can
¼ cup water
1 teaspoon Tomato Paste
¼ teaspoon Nutmeg (optional)
4 to 8 large Shrimp, cleaned
4 large Eggs
¼ cup chopped Fresh Italian Parsley

Season the chicken pieces with salt & pepper, then dredge in flour. Shake off excess flour from chicken. Place Olive Oil in a large frying pan and turn the heat on high. Place chicken in pan and fry over medium-high heat for about 10 minutes until the chicken pieces are nicely browned on all sides.

Remove chicken from pan and set aside. Add onions to pan and cook over low heat for 6 minutes. Add garlic and cook over low heat 2 minutes.

Add Sherry or White Wine to pan and cook on high heat until the liquid is reduced by half. About 4 minutes. As you are cooking the wine, scrape the bottom of the pan with a wooden spoon to dislodge the brown bits on the bottom, which are full of flavor. Add tomatoes to pan and cook at high heat for 4 minutes. Break up the tomatoes a bit with a wooden spoon.

Add chicken back to pan. Add tomato paste, butter, water and nutmeg to pan. Mix. Cover pan, leaving lid slightly ajar. Cook on low heat for 25 to 30 minutes, until the chicken is tender and cooked through.

Divide chicken equally on four plates. Put a breast and wing on two plates, and a leg & thigh on the other two plates. Pour pan juices over the chicken.

Cook the Shrimp in a pan with Olive Oil over medium heat, until the shrimp are cooked through and there is no rawness in the center. About 3 minutes. Place the shrimp in equal portions on plate with chicken.

Fry four eggs the pan you cooked the shrimp in, being careful not to break the yolk. Put one egg on each plate with chicken.

Sprinkle parsley over the chicken and shrimp but not the egg. Serve your guest and have a battle feast meal, just like Napoleon Bonaparte.

CHICKEN TETRAZZINI

Chicken Tetrazzini. This dish is as old-school as they come. It's got a fancy name. Well it was fancy in its day, way back in the 50's and 60's. It's no longer today. "All that fancy, that is." It has virtually disappeared from restaurant menus, in fact it is completely extinct. But you! You can make it at home. Make it for your grandpa or grandma, if you're lucky enough to still have them. It'll bring back memories for them. You'll make them happy, and that in return will make you happy. All over Chicken Tetrazzini! Imagine that?

The RECIPE:

8 ounces Fettuccine Pasta
4 Boneless Chicken Breast
4 tablespoons Olive Oil, 2 Tbs. Butter
12 ounces Button Mushrooms, wash & slice
Salt & Black Pepper
¼ cup Dry White Wine, ½ cup Heavy Cream
¼ teaspoon Nutmeg
½ cup grated Fontina or Swiss Cheese
¼ cup chopped fresh Italian Parsley

Place olive oil and half the butter in a frying pan and heat to medium. Add chicken breast to pan. Sprinkle a little salt & pepper over the chicken breast. Cook on medium heat for 4 minutes.

Turn chicken breast over. Season with this side of chicken breast facing up with salt & pepper. Cook chicken until cooked through, about 3 minutes.

Remove chicken from pan and set aside. Add mushrooms to pan and cook on high heat for 2 to 3 minutes. Season with salt & pepper. Lower heat, and cook for 3 – 4 minutes while stirring with a wooden spoon. Remove from pan and set aside.

Cook fettuccine according to directions on package. Drain, place in a small casserole dish that you'll bake the chicken in. Add 1 tablespoon butter and mix.

Place wine in pan that chicken and mushrooms cooked in. Cook at high heat until wine is reduced by half. About 3 minutes.

Add cream to pan. Add a pinch of salt and pepper, and the nutmeg. Cook on high heat for 5 minutes. Turn off flame.

Spread mushrooms over fettuccine in casserole. Slice chicken and neatly place over the mushrooms. The chicken should be sliced but left in 4 whole pieces sliced. Pour cream over chicken and fettuccine. Sprinkle cheese over the chicken. Bake in a 375 degree oven for 12 minutes. Remove from oven. Place chicken on four plates and sprinkle with Parsley.

UNCLE VINNY'S SAUSAGE & BEANS

This is a quick and easy dish that's quite satisfy. Any good Italian-American loves his Sausage, and can never get enough. This is a preparation that's a little different from the norm and most poplar style of Sausage & Peppers. Uncle Vinny used to make it all the time, and this is his recipe.

12 links Italian Sweet Sausage
1 large Onion, peeled and cut into thick slices
12 tablespoons Olive Oil
6 cloves Garlic, peeled and sliced
2 – 14 ounce cans, Cannellini or Barlotti Beans
½ cup water
2 tablespoons Tomato Paste
¼ cup chopped fresh Parsley (optional)

Place the Sausages in a medium pan with half the olive oil. Cook over medium heat for 10 minutes to brown the sausages nicely.

Add water to cover the sausages and cook at a low simmer for 10 minutes. Remove sausages and set aside.

UNCLE PETE'S BAKED RABBIT
alla Ischiana

1 – 3 to 3 ½ lb. Rabbit cut into 8 pieces
8 medium Button Mushrooms, cut in half
4 Garlic Cloves, peeled and left whole
10 tablespoons Olive Oil
¼ teaspoon course Sea Salt
½ Tbs. Black Pepper
2 Idaho Potatoes,
peeled and cut into large chunks
¼ cup Dry White Wine
¼ cup fresh chopped Italian Parsley
¼ cup grated Pecorino Romano Cheese

Place Rabbit and Olive Oil in a large frying pan and cook the Rabbit over medium heat for 10 minutes. Turn pieces from time to time and brown the rabbit nicely.

Place the rabbit with the olive oil and cooking pan juices into a baking pan with all remaining ingredients. Mix to coat the rabbit, potatoes and mushrooms with oil and juices.

Bake for 15 minutes at 400 degrees. Lower heat and bake for 40 minutes at 325 degrees.

Remove pan from oven. Sprinkle just the rabbit pieces with a little bit each of the Pecorino Cheese. Put in oven and cook at 400 degrees for 8 minutes.

Remove pan from oven and let set for 8 minutes. Place the rabbit with potatoes & mushrooms on to two separate plates. Sprinkle with Parsley and Enjoy!

Discard water from pan. Place remaining oil in the pan the sausages cooked in and add the onions. Cook onions on low heat for 10 minute until the onions are a bit soft and lightly browned. Add garlic and cook on low heat for 3 minutes.

Drain and rinse the beans and add to pan with the onions. Add tomato sauce and ¼ cup of water and cook on medium heat for 3 minutes. Add Sausages and simmer on low heat for 8 minutes.

Serve 4 equal portions of beans and sausages on to 4 plates. Sprinkle with chopped parsley and a drizzle of Olive Oil. Enjoy!

ITALIAN MEATLOAF

RECIPE!

1 cup Breadcrumbs, 1 cup Milk
6 tablespoons Olive Oil
1 large Onion, peeled and finely diced
12 button Mushrooms, sliced
3 cloves Garlic, peeled and minced fine
1 ½ pounds Ground Beef
1 ½ pounds Ground Pork
3/4 cup Tomato Sauce
½ cup chopped fresh Italian Parsley
1 Large Egg, 1 teaspoon dry Oregano
1 teaspoon each of Sea Salt & Black Pepper
half cup grated Parmigiano Reggiano Cheese

Place breadcrumbs and milk in a large bowl and mix. Let stand until needed.

Place mushrooms in a large frying pan and cook with olive oil on high heat for 3 minutes. Add onions and cook 3 minutes. Add garlic, lower heat and cook on low heat for 5 minutes. Turn heat off and let cool to room temperature.

Once the mushrooms and onions have cooled, add to bowl with breadcrumbs. Add ground meats and all remaining ingredients and mix thoroughly with your hands.

Place meat mixture into a Pyrex or Ceramic Baking Meatloaf Pan. Bake in a 325 degree oven for about 1 hour and 15 minutes.

GOULASH al TRIESTINO
Italian Beef Goulash "Yes It's Italian"

Italian Goulash you ask? Yes it's Italian! From Friuli and Trieste in North-Easter Italy, which borders Austria and the area was actually a part of the Austro-Hungarian Empire. The dish is great, the Austrians left, but not the Goulash, and so these Northern Italians are quite lucky. Who doesn't love a good Goulash. Make this recipe, serve with boiled potatoes or over wide egg noodles and you'll be in Heaven. So will your guests. Mangia Bene la Goulash!

INGREDIENTS:

3 pounds of Beef Chuck, cut in 2 ½ " pieces
8 tablespoons Olive Oil
2 large Onions, peeled and cut in large chunks
2 tablespoons Sweet Hungarian Paprika
1 teaspoon dried Oregano
1 teaspoon each of Salt & Black Pepper
5 tablespoons tomato paste
2 tablespoons flour
1 Bay Leaf

Place half the Olive Oil in a medium pot and half in a large frying pan. Brown half the beef in the frying pan and half the beef in the pot. You need to do this so the beef will brown well and not be over-crowded and steam instead of getting nice and brown, which will give the dish a lot of its flavor. Cook over medium to high heat for 15 minutes, turning the pieces of beef as necessary to get all pieces nice and browned.

Add half the onions to the pot and the other half to the frying pan. Cook a medium heat for 5 minutes.

Add half each of the; Paprika, Salt, Pepper, and Oregano to each of the 2 pans. Cook at low heat for 2 minutes.

Place one cup of the water into the frying pan with the beef and turn heat to high. Scrape the bottom of the pan to loosen any brown bits sticking to pan. Cook two minutes. This is deglazing and there's a lot of flavor in those bits on the bottom.

Pour all the beef and onions and every bit of liquid from the frying pan into the larger pot.

Add the Bay Leaf, tomato Paste, and 1 cup of water to the pot. Turn heat to high.

Mix flour into the remaining cup of water and mix thoroughly. Pour this into pot with beef.

Bring to the boil, then lower flame so the goulash is cooking at a slow simmer. Cook for 2 to 2 ½ hours at a slow simmer until the beef is nice and tender. Make sure you stir the goulash from time-to-time with a wooden spoon so it doesn't stick or burn.

Serve Goulash with boiled potatoes or over wide egg noodles if you like. Sprinkle with chopped fresh Parsley and enjoy.

STEAK PIZZAIOLA

There's a scene in the classic 80's movie "The Pope of Greenwich Village" that mentions Steak Pizzaiola. Tony Musante, playing Paulie's (Eric Roberts) Uncle Pete tells Paulie, "where do come off robbin Eddie Grant (Mafia Boss) Paulie? You're a dam Waiter for Christ sake." Because Paulie broke in to Eddie Grants trucking company office and stole a lot of money out of Eddie's safe with his half-Irish cousin Charlie Morrant, played by Mickey Rourke. Paulie asks his Uncle Pete who is in the Mob and in Eddie's Crew, what he thinks the Mafia Boss "Bed Bug Eddie" is going to do to him. Uncle Pete says that he'll probably take a finger. And when Paulie says, "No," in disbelief and horror, Uncle Pete, says, Yeah, and he'll sit down to a Steak Pizzaiola right after." Meaning, chopping off one of his fingers (his Thumb actually) doesn't mean a thing to the Bed Bug, and it won't upset him at all or his appetite.

As many of you may know, The Pope of Greenwich Village is a popular and beloved movie of the Italian-American community, with great performances by; Eric Roberts as Charlie Morrant's dumb blundering cousin Paulie.

Charlie played by Mickey Rourke in what many feel was Mickey's greatest performance. The movie is just great, and if you've never seen it, then you must. Anyway, Steak Pizzaiolo is one of those special treat Italian dishes like Lobster Fra Diavolo or a Veal Chop. Steak, Lobster, and Veal not being cheap, not for everyday consumption, but once-in-a-while for a special treat. Steak Pizzaiola is a favorite of Mob Guys, guys with bent noses and Pinky Rings, "if you know what I mean?" But you don't have to be a Mob Guy to eat one, anyone can. Try making one the way Bed Bug Eddie likes his. The recipe is below.

STEAK PIZZAIOLO
"BED BUG EDDIE STYLE"

4 – 8 oz. Sirloin Steaks, cut 1" thick
¼ cup Red Wine
1 pound Button Mushrooms, washed and sliced
1 tablespoon butter
1 small Onion, peeled and sliced
4 cloves Garlic, peeled and sliced thin
1 teaspoon Dry Oregano
½ teaspoon Red Pepper Flakes
1 – 16 can whole San Marzano Tomatoes
¼ cup fresh Italian Parsley, chopped
¼ cup Olive Oil
Kosher or Sea Salt & Black Pepper

Heat a frying pan that is big enough to hold the 4 steaks.

Add 3 tablespoons of Olive Oil to pan. Add steaks to pan. Season top side of steaks with salt & black Pepper and cook steaks on high heat for 4 minutes. Do not move the steaks as they cook.

Turn steaks over to cook on second side. Season top of steaks with salt & Pepper. Cook steak on high heat for 3 minutes. Remove steaks from pan and set aside in a bowl that is big enough to hold them.

Pour out the fat that is in the pan. Put wine in the pan on high heat and scrape the bottom of the pan with a wooden spoon. This is called deglazing, and there is a ton of flavor in those brown bits on the bottom of the pan. Let cook until the wine reduce by half its original volume. Add 8 tablespoons of water and continue the process until all the liquid reduces by half. Turn off heat and pour the liquid in the bowl with the steaks.

Add 3-tablespoons olive oil to pan. Add the mushrooms and butter to pan. Cook the mushrooms on medium while stirring with a wooden spoon. After they are cooking for 5 minutes, season mushrooms with a little salt & black pepper. Continue cooking about 2 minutes more until nice and brown. Turn heat off and put the mushrooms in the bowl with the steaks.

Put remaining olive oil in pan with the onions. Season onions with salt & pepper. Cook on medium low heat for about 7 minutes. Add garlic and cook for 2 minutes. Add oregano and cook 1 minute.

Make sure you have drained the tomatoes from water in can. Turn heat to high and add tomatoes. Crush the tomatoes with a wooden spoon to break them up a bit. Cook on high heat for two minutes. Add the mushrooms and the liquid in the bowl with the steaks to pan.

Cook tomatoes on medium heat for 6 minutes while stirring, then turn heat to low. Cook for 7 minutes on low heat.

Add steaks back to pan with tomatoes and cook on medium heat for 4 minutes, turning the steaks at the 2 minute point.

Turn heat off, and let set for four minutes.

Add a steak to each of four plates. Pour some sauce over each plate. Sprinkle a little parsley over each steak and a little olive oil if you like. Serve and enjoy.

TONY'S OXTAIL STEW

There aren't many things better than braised oxtails and a nice Oxtail Stew. Oxtails are big in Tuscany and of course in Rome, in the famous Roman dish, Coda d' Vaccinara. This is my Uncle Tony's tasty recipe. Hope you enjoy.

RECIPE:

6 tablespoons Olive Oil
4 pounds Oxtails
2 medium onions, peeled and chopped
5 Garlic Cloves, peeled and sliced
1 ½ cups Dry Red Wine
2 cups Chicken Broth
3 cups water
Kosher or Sea Salt & Black Pepper
4 tablespoons of Tomato Paste
6 Carrots, peeled and slice
4 stalks of Celery, cut in 1 ½ " pieces
1 Bay Leaf
6 tablespoons Butter, softened
¼ cup Flour

Lay the Oxtails out on a cookie pan. Season with Salt and Pepper. Brown Oxtails in batches in a 6 quart pot until they are all golden brown on both sides. Cook the oxtails over medium-high heat about 5 minutes per side. Do not crowd the oxtails, or they won't brown properly. This is why you need to brown them in about 3 batches or so.

Remove the oxtails from pan once they are all brown and let set on the cookie sheet. Add onions and cook over medium heat for 5 minutes. Lower heat. Add garlic and cook for 3 minutes.

Add all the Oxtails to the pot. Add the wine and cook on high heat until wine is reduced by half. Make sure to stir with a wooden spoon, scraping the bottom of the pot to dislodge and brown bits on bottom of the pot.

Add chicken stock, water, bay leaf, and tomato paste to pot. Bring to the boil, then lower to a low steady simmer and let all simmer for 1 ½ hours, stirring occasionally.

After stew has been cooking for 1 ½ hours, add carrots. Cook 30 minutes more.

Thoroughly mix flour and butter in a small bowl. Add to pot little by little, stirring as you do so. Let simmer 30 minutes, stirring occasionally. Oxtails should be nice and tender and ready to eat. Serve with Boiled or Mashed Potatoes, or Polenta.

VEAL STEW alla SCARLOTTA

INGREDIENTS:

2 ½ pounds Veal Stewing Meat, Chuck or Flaps
5 tablespoons olive oil, 1 tablespoon Butter
Salt & Black Pepper
1 medium Onion, peeled and diced
1 pound Button Mushrooms, quartered
2 stalks Celery, diced
2 Carrots, peeled and sliced
½ cup Dry White Wine
3 cups water
3 tablespoons Tomato Paste
1 Bay Leaf
3 tablespoon Cornstarch mixed
with 4 tablespoons water
3 Idaho Potatoes, peeled & cut into
8 large pieces
2 oz. Dry Porcini Mushrooms, reconstituted
10 ounce package Frozen Peas

Cut the Veal into 1 ½ inch cubes.

Place olive oil in a 6 quart no-corrosive pot. Turn heat on to medium pot. Brown the veal on a medium high flame in 2 or 3 batches. Season the veal with salt & pepper as you're browning.

Turn veal every few minutes so all side get nicely brown.

Set veal aside when all of it has been browned. Add onions to pan and cook on medium heat for 4-5 minutes. Add wine and cook until the wine is reduced by half, making sure to scrape the bottom of the put with a wooden spoon to dislodge the brown bits on the bottom (these bits are full of flavor and help make the sauce tasty). Remove onion wine mixture from pot and set aside.

Add butter and button mushrooms to pot. Season with salt & pepper. Cook over medium heat for about 7 minutes until the mushrooms are nicely browned. Remove from pot and set aside.

Add the veal, onions, carrots, bay leaf, tomato paste, water, and reconstituted Porcini Mushrooms to the pot.

Bring all to the boil. Once this has all come to the boil, low flame so the stew is simmering at a low simmer. Cook 1 hour and 15 minutes. Mixing occasionally so stew does not stick and burn.

Add the Cornstarch & Water mixture, mix and cook two minutes.

Add potatoes to pot and continue cooking for 35 minutes. Add peas, cook two minutes. The Stew is ready to serve. Buon Appetito!

NOTE: You can make Beef Stew with this same recipe. Just substitute Beef Chuck for the Veal and cook 30 minutes longer than you cook the Veal.

PEACHES alla LUCIA

My mother used to make this when I was a kid. I can remember my dad bringing home a big bushel basket of ripe summer peaches when they were in season. The basket was so big and with so many peaches that they were too much and my mom would split the peaches with the neighbors who had a large family with lots of kids. I really loved these peaches when I was a boy, and always looked forward to eating them. They were "oh so Yummy." They still are. I had forgotten completely about the peaches and the way my mother used to make them until this past summer when I bought a few fresh peaches from my local Fruit & Vegetable guy on West 4th Street in Greenwich Village. The Peaches smelled good, nice and perfectly ripe. And it hit me! I remembered back to the days my mom used to make them, and one day specifically in our neighbors back yard. The neighbors had a couple of Geese and they were running around the yard. My mom and Mrs. Griffin sat in lawn chairs peeling peaches from the large bushel. I watched them, and watched the Geese. We ate the Peaches, and I can still taste them till this very day.

LUCY'S PEACH SALAD

This recipe is as simple as can be. It's only Peaches and a little sugar. No cooking! The hardest part is getting the rip peaches. Make, it and you'll be amazed at how unbelievably tasty these peaches are. It's great to give to kids, as a much better sweet alternative to super sugar and floured full cakes and cookies. Get the kids hooked on these peaches and tasty Watermelon and Cherries and they might not want too many cakes and cookies. They're fine, but too many are not. Eat healthy.

INGREDIENTS:

12 large ripe Peaches
7 teaspoons of granulated Sugar

Wash the Peaches well. Do not peel. Cut the peaches in half, removing the pit in the center. Cut each half peach into 5 or 6 wedges each and put into a large glass or ceramic bowl that you will serve the Peach Salad from. Once all the peaches are cut up and put into the bowl, add the sugar. Mix thoroughly, then give to your guest and see how much they love it, and how amazed out how tasty and easy this wonderful little dessert is. Buon Appetito!

RICOTTA CHEESECAKE

Ingredients:

2 lbs. whole milk Ricotta
6 extra large Eggs
¾ cup Sugar
zest of 2 Lemon and 1 Oranges
1/8 teaspoon of Salt
1 teaspoon Vanilla Extract
4 tablespoons flour
1-2 cup plain breadcrumbs & 2 tablespoons
Sugar
Butter (to grease pan)

Grease a spring-form pan with butter. Mix bread- crumbs and 2 tablespoons of sugar together. Place mixture in buttered pan. Move breadcrumb mixture around to coat pan with mixture.

Beat eggs with ¾ cup of sugar. Add vanilla, and Lemon & Orange Zest if using. Add flour and continue beating ingredients together. Little by little, add the Ricotta to bowl and mix until all the ricotta is incorporated and smooth.

Heat oven to 375 degrees.

Place the spring-form pan inside a large pan. Pour all of the Ricotta (Cheesecake) mixture inside the spring-form pan. Pour warm water into the larger pan that is holding the spring-form pan with the ricotta mixture. Pour water half way up the sides of the spring-form pan. This is a water-bath.

Bake for 15 minute at 370 degrees. Turn oven down to 325 degree and bake cheesecake for 50 to 60 minutes more, until when you put a toothpick into the center of the cake, it comes out clean.

Cool cheesecake for 1 hour outside at room temperature. Place cheesecake in refrigerator and cook for 2 to 3 hours before serving.

CUCIDATI "Sicilian Fig Cookies"

For COOKIE DOUGH:

1/3 cup Granulated Sugar
1 ½ cups All Purpose Flour
1/4 teaspoon baking powder
1/2 cup vegetable shortening
2 tablespoons butter
1/2 cup milk
1 Egg, beaten
1 1/2 cups dried figs
3/4 cup Golden Raisins
1/4 cup Slivered Almonds
1/4 cup white sugar
1/4 cup hot water
1/4 teaspoon ground cinnamon
1 pinch ground black pepper

For SUGAR GLAZE:

1 cup Confectioners Sugar
4 tablespoon Milk, ¼ teaspoon Vanilla Extract
¼ cup Multi Colored Non-Pareil-Candy Sprinkles

In a large mixing bowl, combine flour, 1/3 cup sugar and baking powder. Cut in shortening and butter until mixture resembles small peas. Stir in the milk and egg until the dough comes together. Divide dough into two pieces, wrap and refrigerate for about 1 hour or until easy to handle.

In a food processor or blender, grind the figs, raisins and almonds until they are coarsely chopped. In a medium bowl, stir together the 1/4 cup of sugar, hot water, cinnamon and pepper. Stir in the fruit mixture, cover and set aside until the dough is ready.

Preheat oven to 350 degrees F (175 degrees C). On a lightly floured surface, roll each piece of the dough out to a 12 inch square.

Cut each piece into 12 - 3x4 inch rectangles. Using a heaping tablespoon of filling for each rectangle, spread filling along one of the short sides of the rectangle. Roll up from that side. Place rolls, seam side down, on an un-greased cookie sheet. Curve each roll slightly. Snip outer edge of the curve three times.

Bake for 20 to 25 minutes in a 350 degree oven, until golden brown. Let Cookies cool.

Place confectioners sugar with milk and vanilla in a small bowl and mix with a wooden spoon until thoroughly mixed and smooth.

Coat each cookie with the sugar glaze and sprinkle on some of the Colored Non Pareil Sprinkles. Serve.

ORANGE OLIVE OIL CAKE
alla Sorrentino

Oranges and Olive Oil are along with; wine and tomatoes the lifeblood of the Peninsular of Sorrento and the Amalfi Coast. This is a tasty cake make with two of those essential Campanian ingredients; Olive Oil and Oranges. They make this cake in the beautiful little city of Sorrento where it is loved by both tourists and locals alike. It's not well know in the U.S., but that shouldn't stop you from eating this wonderful cake. Made with olive oil, it's much healthier than a cake made with butter, but equally tasty. "Try it, you'll not like it. You'll Love it!"

RECIPE: Orange Olive Oil Cake

2 cups All Purpose Flour
1 ¾ cups Sugar
1 ½ teaspoons Salt
¾ teaspoons each: Baking Powder & Baking Soda
1 ¼ cup Olive Oil (not Extra Virgin, it's too strong)
1 ½ cups whole Milk, 3 large Eggs
zest from 2 Oranges
¼ cup Fresh Squeezed Orange Juice
4 tablespoons Gran Marnier Liquor

Mix all dry ingredients in a large glass bowl, the; flour, sugar, salt, Baking Powder and Baking Soda.

Mix remaining ingredients in a separate bowl and mix thoroughly with a wire-whip.

Slowly add half of the dry ingredients to the bowl with eggs. Mix slowly and gently folding the two together. Add remaining dry ingredients and mix gently.

Heat oven to 350 degrees. Grease a 9" round cake pan with some softened butter or olive oil.

Pour cake batter in pan. Bake for about 30 minutes, until when you put a toothpick in the center of cake and it comes out clean without any wet batter. It's done.

Let cool for 15 minutes before serving. Sprinkle with powdered sugar and serve.

May be heated before serving. May be served with a little Vanilla Ice Cream on the side or with mixed berries, however it is perfect all on its own with or without the powdered sugar on top. Buon Appetito!

BASTA !!!

"Mille Grazia," (many Thanks) for getting this book. I hope you have enjoyed it and the recipes in it. And hope that you will try and cook, and love these recipes, there's a lot of goodies in there. Whether you are an experienced cook or someone just starting out, you are sure to find something new, that you might never have seen, like; Spare Rib Soup, Pasta alla Generosa, and Pasta con Gallina, all amazing recipes and quite rare, and something new. Then there are all the most popular favorites of the Italian-American Kitchen. Dishes like; Shrimp Cocktail, Fettuccine Alfredo (and al Lemone), Spaghetti & Meatballs, Sunday Sauce aka Gravy, Marinara, Minestrone, and many more.

Finally, there are the Secret Recipes (Segreto Ricette), of which these, though few, are monumental. Like my famed Bolognese Sauce, which is quite renowned, and of which publications like the Journal of Italian Food and Wine said of mine, "It is quite possibly the best Bolognese in the country." That's one of several accolades over the years that I'm quite proud of. When I first wrote this recipe into a cookbook, I was majorly torn. It was mine, and it was famous, "should I give the secret recipe away," just like that? The answer, obviously came down to be yes, which was quite the difficult decision, but I did, so there you go. Likewise for my *secret recipe* for Eggplant Caponata, another of my dishes that I've been quite well known for over the years, in my former restaurant, the 1st Venetian Wine Bar (Bacaro) in America, one *Bar Cichetti*. I have not yet divulged my secret pasta recipe for Sugo di Anatra (Duck Ragu), but that's for another day. I figured out and replicated the famed sauce Salsa Segrete of our beloved old Red-Sauce Joint, Gino's that sadly closed a few years back. And how both my cousin Joe (Macari) and I miss that place so. It was the perfect old-school Italian-American restaurant, and I along with thousands of others sure do miss it. But "here it is," in this book. After I figured it out, made it, and replicated the taste to perfection, I have written it down. So, you have this book, you have the recipe.

So again, I hope you have enjoyed this book. I enjoyed writing it. Hope you try as many of the recipes as you like, keep the book in your library, and as with any of my books, I hope you will refer to it now and then and tell your friends and family about, the favorite dishes and *Secrets* within. Segreto Italiano. Mangia Bene!

BY THE SAME AUTHOR

SUNDAY SAUCE
1 BEST SELLER AMAZON

La TAVOLA
Italian-American
New Yorkers
Adventures of The Table

THE FEAST of THE 7 FISH
Italian Christmas

GOT ANY KAHLUA?
The Collected Recipes of The Dude
a.k.a. The BIG LEBOWSKI COOKBOOK

Made in United States
North Haven, CT
09 May 2024

52340603R00125